A PRIMER OF
PUBLIC ADMINISTRATION

A PRIMER OF
PUBLIC ADMINISTRATION

by

S. E. FINER, M.A.
Fellow of Balliol College
Oxford

FREDERICK MULLER LIMITED
LONDON

FIRST PUBLISHED BY FREDERICK MULLER LTD
IN 1950
PRINTED AND MADE IN GREAT BRITAIN BY
BILLING AND SONS LTD., GUILDFORD AND LONDON AND
THE LEIGHTON-STRAKER BOOKBINDING CO. LTD LONDON

Second Impression, 1957
Third Impression, October 1961

CONTENTS

FOR
ANN

PREFACE

IN this little book I have tried to describe the principles which underlie Public Administration in this country. It is not strictly a primer in the sense that a primer introduces the subject to a reader who has never considered the matter before. Rather does it represent an attempt to discern the pattern and principles lying behind what usually appears as a tangle of unrelated facts, hidden away in Blue Books or in odd corners of constitutional treatises. I wanted, in short, to attempt a synoptic view of the salient features in the British machinery of government.

As it was written I was forced to sacrifice criticism to analysis, analysis to description and all three to space. All have suffered, but I hope that a rough proportion has been struck. Furthermore a book so short on a subject so vast must entail intellectual pillage on a huge scale. The problem, then, was to select the best booty, and to label it in tidy parcels.

In an era of controls and regulations the study of public administration (which is really a study of the principles on which administrators may be supposed to work) becomes an unusually controversial topic. Let me confess then with Jonathan Swift, and say:

"I would hide the frailties and deformities of my political mother, and place her virtues and beauties in the most advantageous light..."

ACKNOWLEDGMENTS

I OWE a great debt to those many friends and colleagues who read the MS. so carefully and helped so much with their detailed criticisms and their luminous commentary. I wish to express my most sincere thanks to them all: to my brother, Professor Herman Finer of Chicago University, to Mr E. T. Williams of Balliol College, Professor Mackenzie of Manchester University, and Mr R. L. Hall, Fellow of Trinity College Oxford and Director of the Economic Section of the Cabinet Secretariat; to Sir Andrew McFadyean; and by no means the least, to the Master of Balliol, Lord Lindsay of Birker. They will find their wisdom studded throughout the pages of this book; the many errors they discover in them, are all, alas, my own.

S. E. FINER

BALLIOL COLLEGE
18 October 1949

BOOK I

THE ADMINISTRATIVE REVOLUTION

CHAPTER 1

CENTRAL DIRECTION AND CONTROL

"... sets up to be an universal Reformer and Corrector of Abuses, a Remover of Grievances, rakes into every Slut's corner of Nature, bringing hidden corruptions to the light, and raises a mighty dust where there was none before...."

Swift: A Meditation upon a Broomstick.

I

THE first half of the twentieth century has witnessed an administrative revolution.

The nineteenth century saw England with a peculiar and distinctive system of administration. It was everywhere contrasted with that of France which represented its exact antithesis. Whereas the British civil service was run till 1870 by amateurs recruited by patronage France had had her great professionals since the Revolution. Nearly all the British public bodies, for example the local councils, the Universities and the Churches enjoyed a sort of autonomous and equal status, where France organized them in a legal hierarchy with a formal pattern. In Britain each new social service was, with very few exceptions, entrusted to the local authorities,[1] and a whole area of social life, that of the Universities and Schools, the Bar and Medicine, Art and Literature, was left to free voluntary activity. Only in France could a Napoleon blame his Minister of the Interior for the fact that the Empire had no literature! There Education, Justice, the very Church itself came within the control of the State, if not indeed under its active direction. Furthermore not only were British local authorities entrusted with functions which France considered national: until the turn of the century, they were almost entirely autonomous, while those in

[1] The great change was inaugurated by the 1911 precedent by which National Health Insurance was administered by a Central Commission and not by Municipalities.

France were almost powerless. French administration was professional, hierarchical, *étatiste*. It was rigorously centralized. The shape of British administration if "shape it could be called which shape had none, distinguishable in member, form or limb," was haphazard, because amateur. There was no obvious pyramid of control: the State did little, voluntary and local bodies whatever was done; and British local government was autonomous, variegated and thriving.

Neither State much occupied itself with economic problems. Paradoxically Britain was first in the field with her factory inspection, of 1833. But even by 1900, economic activity was regarded as "private" administration in both states, and Adam Smith's "hidden hand," not the State's, was trusted with its negotiation. Although one could discern a "disintegration" of the central government in both countries, i.e. a separate autonomous status for each government department, this was not then a matter of importance. The State was primarily a machine for doling out security and justice and for absorbing revenue. Its positive functions, even in France, were minute compared with what the following half century was to bring.

In the last 50 years the English tradition has been revolutionized, and even the U.S.A., which with its spoils, its federalism, and its passion for private enterprise, *caricatured* the salient features of Great Britain, has moved with her towards the French pattern. In both countries State activity has vastly expanded: this activity is no longer left farmed out to States, local councils, or private associations, but is undertaken, more and more exclusively, by the central agencies of Government.

These trends are epitomized by the growth of Civil Services and in the proportions of national incomes spent by Government agencies. The French central civil service has risen from 90,000 in 1841 to just over 1 million in 1946, i.e. it is 11 times as big—for a population almost the same size. The U.K. has expanded its civil service from some 17,000 in 1841, to 711,000 in 1949: it is some 40 times as large for a population that has increased $2\frac{1}{2}$ times in the same period. The U.S.A. has expanded its civil service by some 100 times for a population that has increased eightfold. And this represents the *central* civil service only! The percentages of national income spent by public agencies tell the same story. In 1913 France was spending only 6.2 per cent, the U.S.A. only 8.4 per cent, Britain only 11.86 per cent. By 1946 France spent 22.7 per cent,

U.S.A. 29.4 per cent, and Britain no less than 37.3 per cent! Every third shilling in the country is managed by a public agency.[1]

Now this is not all. Public authorities are doing more than ever—so much is clear. But the central departments are doing most of this "more". In France in 1913, the local government budgets formed 33.25 per cent of the central expenditures. In 1946 they had fallen to 13.83 per cent. In the U.S.A. in 1910 the total of State and local budgets together was approximately 200 per cent of the total Federal (central) expenditures. In 1946 it had fallen to 50 per cent. In Great Britain, the local councils spent, in 1910, an aggregate sum equal to 54 per cent of that laid out by the Central Departments. By 1946, that proportion had fallen to some 20 per cent, only half of which was raised locally.

These striking developments have gone together with a changed pattern of administration. In all three countries the administration has become increasingly professional. It is organized in a pyramid of authority, a hierarchy. The dominant pattern is centralization, not the autonomy of voluntary or "private" associations. The State undertakes an ever widening range of services, and the departments of state which administer them are co-ordinated to make a single unified structure.

This is the revolution. Why has it happened? And what problems has it raised?

II

It may be deplorable that individuals do less and less and the State more and more. But a purely personal analysis of a great world trend is liable to concentrate attention on the inessential. Perhaps some civil servants *are* power hungry and "empire builders"; but so, it is boasted, are business men.Why has the first encroached on the sphere of the second? Why has success lain with the civil servant? It was not always so. In the nineteenth century in Great Britain and Europe generally, the business man triumphed and broke down the mercantilist barriers of the eighteenth century. Unless the underlying causes of our administrative revolution are

[1] Military expenditure accounts for a large part of their increase. France spent 4.2 per cent of her national income on defence in 1913 compared with 7.7 per cent in 1946. Britain's percentage rose from 2 per cent in 1913 to about 13 per cent in 1946.

discovered, no appreciation of the real problems of administration can be attempted.

This revolution was caused by four main factors. In the first place the last half century had seen the rise of organized labour. It began with a sort of distributive socialism, a demand that wages be the first charge on industry, and reformist socialism has retained this characteristic ever since. To realize such a programme implies not only State control of hours, conditions and wages—it may in the last resort imply State operation of the industry, i.e. the entire elimination of the profits and rents charge on industry. It may even entail subsidizing the industry at the community's expense. Hence labour has been openly State interventionist from the outset. The two great wars of our time and the Great Depression emphasized its claims, the wars because they enhanced labour's organizing and bargaining powers, the depression because it intensified the demand for security and a national minimum standard of living.

As labour organized, so capital concentrated. Even in the U.K. 2,000 firms employ over half of the total labour force. The British businessman became less and less a free trader as Germans, Americans and Japanese invaded first his foreign and then his home markets. The Great Depression of 1929 completed the rout of economic liberalism. No longer protective tariffs alone, but subsidies, bounties, "schemes" of all kinds were the order of the day. The wars demanded certain measures of protection; for even Adam Smith had claimed that "defence was greater than opulence". The Great Depression sounded the *sauve qui peut* of all the capitalists in the world, and when the disastrous rout was over, the novel peace of Economic Nationalism reigned all over the battle field. Private Enterprise stood all lined up and bright as a new made pin: *at the expense of the tax-payer.*

Thus both the traditional "Right" and "Left" were interventionist in the period of the two wars. Economic liberalism was squeezed out between these giant organized forces, caught "between the fell incensed points of mighty opposites". Henceforth, i.e. from 1929, *Laissez-faire* had lost its clientele and the great public issue was no longer for or against State intervention but rather whose interest, that of capital or labour, should intervention serve?

A third trend was the ever increasing sub-division of labour. Every locality became less and less self sufficient, more and more dependent on the economic and social ease of the economy as a whole. A disturbance, a flood, a strike in one corner of Britain, affected every other part. The internal security of the State, peace and order, fire and flood prevention, became an increasing social concern. To-day the Police establishment of Britain and Wales is some 66,000[1] and some complain it is too few. In 1839 the *maximum* estimate for the numbers required ran to 8,000 only.[2]

The social division of labour also meant the elaboration of more and more stages of manufacture that productive processes were endlessly multiplied and chopped up. This "roundabout" nature of production again demanded State interference. The interruption of one stage in the process spelt dislocation of whole industries, the unbearable absence of thousands of vital commodities from the shops. Increasingly strikes and lock-outs demand to be either crushed or arbitrated; so collective bargaining was reinforced by the active interest of the State, by the Whitley Council movement, the Arbitration Boards; and behind the show of benevolent interest, there went a threat of force, of D.O.R.A. and The Defence Regulations. Again, as production became more and more "social", interests became increasingly sectional. Not only did Capital struggle with Labour but whole industries, manufacture and agriculture, import and export, light and heavy industry struggled among themselves, all trying to grasp a larger share of the national product and to beggar its neighbour. The turmoil was reflected back in the new aspect of the State. As divider, planner, regulator of the national product, it tried to balance those rival claims and, in doing so, to temper expediency with justice.

The demands of Capital, of Labour, and indeed of industrialism itself have together constituted the modern tremendous cumulative drive towards State intervention.

But it is a peculiar *form* of intervention: it is centralized. This peculiarity derives from a fourth and final cause operating in the last half century: the shrinkage of administrative space. The internal combustion engine, bringing with it the automobile and aeroplane, and the development of telecommunications have together revolutionized *space*. The life of a community is no longer self regarding or "local", and distance as a barrier of effective control has disappeared. Units like the counties which in 1890 were still, administratively speaking, as wide as in William the Conqueror's day, had by 1946 shrunk to ciphers. It is easier to-day to administer England

[1] Ann. Abs. Stats. No. 84, 1948, Table 46.

[2] Constab. Rept. 1839, §243. Cf. Halévy, *Clio aux Enfers*, for a description of the same tendency in France.

from London than it was to administer Oxfordshire from Oxford forty years ago.

The growth of State Activity and its centralizing tendencies do not then derive from a sinister plot by a wicked internationale of government employees nor the caprice of legislators. It springs from the social and economic demands made by people in the last half century. It cannot be cured by halving the Civil Service any more than the tides receded for King Canute. It can only be misunderstood, and therefore mishandled by merely labelling it, the "New Despotism" and "Road to Serfdom". It may be reconciled with freedom and individuality only by understanding its nature. Only when we know why, what and how can we control and guide. Indeed, the impact of this secular movement towards State intervention has created problems for the public service which are novel, difficult, and still largely unsolved even in theory. Yet solved they must be.

III

These problems arise from two main sources, the impact of size and mass, and the *direction* of activity. These cause problems in so far as they affect the expression of *public will*, and the machinery of executing it, viz. of *public administration*.

In a modern democracy the public will is *formally* expressed through a Legislature, in this country through Parliament.[1] The impact of Size and Mass on legislatures has been profound.

The first effect of size on legislatures is that the individual has been removed further and further from a personal share in policy making. The democracy of the market place, of Athens, has disappeared. Rousseau's general meeting of citizens takes place to-day only in a few public spirited rural parishes. Representative democracy supplants direct democracy and for representative democracy to work there must be political parties to inform, educate, and organize the electorate, and pressure groups to defend the interests of individual groups. Yet these themselves become so large that the individual member of either is more and more at the mercy of the local committee and the local committee itself at the mercy of the central committee. More and more stages separate the individual from the determination of policy. In the last resort, he can only

[1] I stress *formally*, because in practice it is expressed through a myriad voluntary associations and pressure groups.

assert himself by voting with his feet!—he bolts his party, his Union, his association, his church. Hence the plethora of devices to overcome this situation and provide an "ersatz" of direct democracy:— the Recall and the Referendum, the Parliaments of Industry and the Corporate State, Mass Observation, Peace Ballots and Gallup Polls. Now, not only has Parliament become remote from the common voters, but its work has enormously increased. There are the same numbers in the Commons, perhaps a better but not greatly better quality. But there are still only 24 hours in the day, and the amount of legislation, however, has nearly trebled since 1909.[1] Hence the much bemoaned features of modern parliamentary procedure, the reduction of discussion by closure and the guillotine, the increased use of Standing Committees and Sub-Committees, the development of skeleton legislation and inevitably, an increased rule-making power to the Government departments.

The impact of *size* on Society has caused great problems in focusing and finding out what is the public will; but the *direction* of its activity has created problems still more startling: and it is primarily out of these that the difficulties of public administration spring.

The central government has absorbed three main types of activity. It has undertaken once voluntary activities; it has also undertaken many former functions of local authorities, and finally a section previously regarded as somehow inherently immune, namely "private" (economic) enterprise has been either absorbed, directed, or controlled. Looking at the administrative aspect alone, economic enterprise is no more distinctive than church schools or local utilities. It is simply an extraordinarily decentralized section of public administration. Whether Mr B., a baker, bakes bread, is his own affair. Whether many bakers refuse to bake bread is a public affair. Any private economic interest may be "affected with a public interest".[2] The limits of public control of *any* private activity economic or otherwise, are, to the administrator, matters of sheer expediency.

In each of these three cases the problem of the administrator is this: by virtue of his public and central status he can render the public certain services which the existing agency fails to provide, but he may thereby destroy certain values peculiar to the former agency.

[1] 3rd Report, Select Committee of House of Commons on Procedure, 1946, p. vi.

[2] Cf. Munn *v.* Illinois, 1876; 94 U.S 113, 24 Law Ed. 77. Quoted Evans, *Cases on Constitutional Law*, Callaghan & Co., Chicago, 1933, p. 1128.

His problem is not to offset the gains and losses of public against private enterprises. There must be *no* losses. His problem is the provision of substitutes.

For example, when a Ministry itself administers a service formerly undertaken by local authorities, it replaces by a national standard the former variety of local standards, it makes universal provision where previously provision may have been patchy and localized, and it can operate within technically ideal areas. A great deal however may be lost. The council's knowledge of its area and people may be lost; so may the incentives of local patriotism; so also the speedy, easy accountability of local government officers to the local rate-payer. What is a Ministry to substitute for these? Similarly when a Ministry undertakes work formerly performed by a private "voluntary" agency, it justifies its action by any or all of the following arguments: it may claim that it makes provision universal instead of partial, that its standard is national and uniform instead of varying with the excellence of the private association, that its administration is economical instead of being expensively redundant, that its service is full time and professional rather than amateur. These are valid justifications: but there are defects in their qualities. Professional paid service is not the same as an ardent missionary spirit. Universal provision precludes special attention for "deserving" cases. A universal standard implies that none may be turned away and what might be a high standard of service for a limited number may degenerate into a mediocre standard for all, simply because the administration is swamped by numbers. Not the Highest Common Factor is provided, but the Lowest Common Denominator.

These considerations are perhaps most noticeable where a private economic enterprise is nationalized. Profit and competition are no longer an incentive or a criterion. What is to replace them? The producer may no longer discriminate between one customer and another, he cannot choose his own clientèle. Service becomes *average*, uniform. There are no valleys of incompetence or slovenliness—but neither are there peaks of imagination and forethought. The consumer, unless he is afflicted with a monopoly, may always "vote with his pay packet", by taking his custom elsewhere. How can he guarantee that quality, price and product are what he really demands when he is *served by a State monopoly*?[1]

The Central Government then, claims to give provision that is

[1] Cf. Electricity Bill, Recommitted to House, Hansard, 24th, 25th, 26th June, 1947.

16

universal, and of a minimum standard, and to achieve the economies of large scale enterprise. But in the transfer of responsibilities, certain losses may occur. To summarize them from the considerations above, we first have the losses of *knowledge*—local knowledge, or, in the case of economic enterprises, technical knowledge and "Know How". Then come the losses of *incentive*—it may be the crusading spirit of a voluntary hospital, the local pride of a municipality, the profit motive of the private firm. Finally some *accountability* may be lost—the voluntary association is responsible to its members, indeed it consists of its members, the local council is in intimate touch with a local electorate and the Town Hall within easy grumbling distance, the private firm is controlled by the sovereignty of the consumer. Somehow all these losses must be made good, by adequate substitutes. Yet the very qualities of a Ministry—universality of provision and standard—make such substitution very difficult: for, making universal provision, the agency cannot discriminate— it must ration its quality and quantity of service in accordance with the numbers who claim it; and because it is a public agency, and hence regulated by a written law or charter within which it must act,[1] it is denied the chance of free initiation, risk taking, and spontaneity! The difficulty is precisely this: we may praise "universal provision" and "minimum standards": we may decry "indiscriminate (or wasteful) provision" and "*average* standards". Yet both sets of terms refer to the identical matter. To those hitherto underendowed in respect to some service, the levelling, averaging process will seem an improvement, a levelling *upwards*. To those hitherto overendowed, it will seem a destruction of excellency, a reduction to mediocrity. And both are right, for both reflect the essence of State provision—it is and *must* be average. After all an average is only another way of expressing a ration, or equality, of treatment. So State activity is like Mother Sereda, who bleaches everything white, who presides over Wednesdays, the middle day of the week, "the factor of middleness, of mediocrity, of an avoidance of extremes—".[2] The Civil Service is the Mother Sereda of the modern age.

Thus the *direction* of State activity has affected the nature and expression of public *will*, institutionalized as it is in parties, Parliament, and the Civil Service. The influence of the size of the modern State and the direction of its activity upon the *execution* of policy

[1] See below pp. 132 *et seq.*
[2] Branch Cabell, *Jurgen* (Bodley Head, 1932), p. xiv.

follows from these considerations. Since it takes over activities which were formerly self regulating (i.e. local activities, voluntary activities, private firms) it raises the problem of the accountability of ministries and corporations to the public, through the Courts and through Parliament. Because these activities were formerly performed by enthusiasts, fanatics, specialists or profiteers, it raises the problem of the recruitment, training and incentives of public servants. Because so much demands specialist knowledge, the provision of expertness and science becomes a pressing question. Upon a set of government agencies already perplexed by these difficulties bursts the impact of *size*. On what principles are all these multifarious duties to be divided between the different ministries and agencies? This is the problem of "departmentalization". And, having once divided the work between them how are these separate agencies to be made to work together?

These, then, are the problems which are specific to a study of public administration:

1. The machinery of co-ordination.
2. The principles of departmentalization.
3. The accountability of the executive to Courts and Parliament.
4. The provision of expert knowledge.
5. The recruitment and maintenance of qualified personnel in the public service.

Administration does not, however, operate in a vacuum; it is *instrumental*, the *agent* of public policy, of public will. One major feature of the last half century has been the apparent decline of Legislatures which focus the public will, relative to the Executive, which implements it. The initiation of policy seems more and more to pass to the Executive. The relations between the master and the servant, the public will and the executive agency have shifted. Has the axe really boasted itself against him that hewed therewith, and the rod shaken itself against those who lifted it up?[1]

[1] Isaiah, x. 15.

CHAPTER 2

THE SEPARATION OF POWERS

"The fashion of jumbling fifty things together in a Dish, was at first introduced in compliance to a depraved and debauched appetite, as well as to a crazy Constitution."

Swift: A Tale of a Tub.

ONE of the most marked symptoms of the administrative revolution is the rise of administrative leadership, the executive's "invasion" of what has hitherto been regarded as the province of Legislature and Judiciary. By no means confined to this country, it is true also of France, of U.S.A., indeed of all industrialized countries: in all of them the Bar Associations and the traditionalists claim to see in this development one of the major manifestations of the Great Bureaucratic Plot.

This traditionalist analysis tends to obscure the significance of what is really happening. The observed *fact* is that the traditional relationship of the executive to Parliament and the Law Courts is subtly changing. Hitherto the executive was regarded as a mere instrument, a machine, animated by Parliaments and regulated by the Courts. Its discretion was *nil*. In England this role was justified by Dicey's slogans, the Sovereignty of Parliament and the Rule of Law. In the U.S.A. it was set down in black and white by the Constitution of 1789. In France this theory outran practice until the end of the nineteenth century. In every case, the theoretical justification of this relationship derives from an older and justly famous theory—Montesquieu's doctrine, "The Separation of Powers". This doctrine treats of the nature of administrative action, and its difference from other types of state action.

I

Montesquieu's classic work, *L'esprit des Lois*, was published in 1748, yet another of the major unread works of the western intelligence. It is one of the first attempts at a modern Sociology of Law. In Book XI, Chapter VI, the author treats of "The Constitution of England". It was the England of George II, admired for its freedom and liberties by the Baron of Montesquieu living under the despotism of Louis XV. Liberty was in Montesquieu's view, the genius and the passion of the English: and he claimed that the

Constitution guaranteed it by formalizing a peculiar relationship between the Executive, the Legislature and the Law Courts. These three "departments" he claimed, were balanced in equipoise the one against the other. Generalizing from this he propounded the celebrated and evergreen theory that only by such a balance or "separation" could personal liberty be secured.

"In every State, there are three kinds of powers: legislative power, the executive power which relates to international law and the executive power which relates to civil law.

By the first, the prince or magistrate makes *laws*, temporary or permanent and corrects or abrogates those which are in existence. By the second, he makes peace or war, sends or receives ambassadors, establishes security, takes precautions against invasions. By the third he punishes crimes or judges the differences of private persons. We shall call the last the power of adjudication and the other simply the executive power of the State . . .

When legislative and executive power are united in the same person or governing body, there can be no freedom; for you may well fear that that same monarch or senate makes tyrannical laws only to execute them tyrannically.

Nor is there freedom where the power to adjudicate is not separated from the legislative power and the executive power. Conjoined with legislative power, power over the life and liberty of citizens would be arbitrary: for the judge would be making his own laws! Conjoined with the executive power, the judge might have the powers of an oppressor.

All would be lost if the same man or same body of dignitaries or nobles or commoners exercised these three powers: that of making laws, executing the public will and judging the crimes and differences of private persons . . ."

The three powers then must be separated, exercised by different individuals in such a way as to act as checks and balances upon one another:

"These three powers might fall into repose or inactivity. But since they are forced to move by the necessary movement of affairs, they will be forced to move *together*."[1]

Restated, this theory makes three propositions, viz. (i) there are three different *kinds* of *government decisions*, (ii) when all are made by the same agency, a tyranny results, and (iii) hence each of

[1] *L'Esprit des Lois*, Librairie Garnier edn. Book XI, Chap. VI.

the three government agencies, Legislative, Executive and Courts, must make only its own peculiar kind of decision and never trespass upon the province of another agency.

Now the question with which this chapter is concerned bears only on the first proposition, the one that tries to define the nature of administrative action. The second and third positions can be broadly defended and justified without arguing that there are different "kinds" of governmental activity at all. It seems advisable to show this before turning to the main question.

In the United States an act of government requires the concurrence of three bodies, co-ordinate with one another, viz. the Presidency, the Congress, and the Supreme Court. This arrangement was arrived at in explicit deference to the authority of Montesquieu.[1] Its object was to prevent the tyranny not only of any one man or body of men, such as Montesquieu had envisaged, but also the "tyranny of the majority". "A representative assembly", wrote Adams in 1786, "if you give them *all* the power, legislative, executive and judicial .. would invade the liberties of the people; at least the majority of them would invade the liberties of the minority, sooner and oftener than any absolute monarch."[2] "If angels were to govern men," wrote Madison, "neither external nor internal controls on government would be necessary." Their "defect of better motives" then, must be supplied by making the ambition of one authority work against the ambition of another, "the interest of the man" must be connected with "the constitutional rights of the place".

So the "powers" (whatever they may be) were separated. But this arrangement does not demand any theory that government carries out three main activities all of which must be kept separate. It simply requires one to show that any act of government should emanate, not from the decision of one single individual or office, but from the concurrence of several, each independent of its fellows; that, for example, justice should be rendered not by a single magistrate but by a bench of judges. It could be as well served by quite an arbitrary set of offices, separated on quite arbitrary principles, as for example a British constitution in which the Crown, the Peers and the Commons could all veto the actions of one another.

The justification of such checks and balances has nothing to do with the existence of any alleged "three powers". It is simply the

---

[1] *L'Esprit des Lois. Ibid.*

[2] Adams, 1786, quoted in *"Basic Issues of American Democracy"* (Bishop and Hendel), p. 112.

physicians' practice of calling for a "second opinion" enwrapped in the mantle of political institutions. The individual or the minority with a case which they think is good, find it easier to get the benefit of the doubt where the decision that may damn them is not entrusted to one single person or office but to the concurring opinions of several. The tax-payer who is a "border-line case" finds it better considered if he can appeal past the Inland Revenue Authorities to the courts of law or to his Member of Parliament.

And, as a matter of fact, the division of governmental power between three agencies by no means exhausts its long catalogue of divisions in the United States. For the Legislative power is itself divided against itself, into a Senate and a lower House, both artfully and consciously designed to be independent of one another. In addition this woefully self-divided Federal Government possesses only a limited number of functions, the rest falling within the province of the several State governments themselves even more self-divided than the Federal: so that, as *The Federalist* puts it "a double security arises to the rights of the people. The different governments will control each other at the same time that each will be controlled by itself".[1]

To put the matter another way: the "separation of Powers" in the sense described is merely one of a series of possible devices to introduce what might be called an "artificial friction" into the governmental machine. Quick and efficient government will no doubt demand a machine that responds easily and completely to the directing impulse: but where one has some doubts as to the wisdom of such impulses perhaps it is as well to have a machine that falters sufficiently long for the operator to change his mind. There are many devices to produce this result, to slow down and impair the too great resolution and effectiveness of government: Bills of Rights which the courts will enforce, Second Chambers, Referendums and Initiatives, Local Self-Government—all these exemplify the same principle. Montesquieu's "Checks and balances" does not need to rely upon the proposition that there are "three kinds of power" and neither more nor less.

II

This chapter's main problem still remains to be answered. Are there "three kinds of power" such as Montesquieu describes? He

[1] *The Federalist* (Everyman Edition), p. 266. Cf also W. Wilson, *Congressional Government*, Boston, 1889, pp. 12-13.

seems to talk as though what are called Laws, Court Orders and Administrative rulings differed from one another inherently by their *content*. If this were so one could scrutinize the various activities of government, classify them under one of these three heads and refer them as particularly appropriate to a particular department of state. This is in fact what the Supreme Court of the U.S.A. sometimes has to do. It must ensure that no one department of the Government exercises the functions which properly, under the Constitution, belong to the other departments. This involves it in deciding, in the most particular and concrete cases, whether a certain matter is Judicial, Legislative or Administrative.[1]

The activities of government do not however differ inherently by their content. They differ by virtue of the agency undertaking them. A law is a decision arrived at by Parliament, a court decision is one arrived at by the Courts an administrative rule is one arrived at by a Department. This truism illustrates the point: it is not true that the content of particular acts decides the technique and scope of the three types of governmental agency—it is the width of discretion and the technique peculiar to each of the three types of government agency that decides whether the particular subject matter that any one may promulgate possesses the characteristic flavour and appearance of legislative, judicial or administrative decision.

Laws differ from administrative or judicial decisions in the first place because the discretion of the legislature is an unlimited one. It may regulate the water rate of Bootle or sanction the Defence Regulations. The point is not the generality of the law's provision, but the generality of the Legislature's power to make *any* kind of decision whatsoever. This is what Carré de Malberg means when he writes:

"for a rule to be legislative, it is indispensible and also sufficient that it is the handiwork of the legislative power, i.e. the organ in which that power exclusively rests. The notion of law is thus independent of any condition bearing upon the content of the legislative act. It is a notion ... of a purely formal order: for it is conditioned only by the origin of the act, by the quality of its author and the form of its adoption."[2]

[1] W. Gellhorn, *Administrative Law* (Foundation Press Inc.), Chapters 2 & 3.

[2] Quoted *Précis de Droit Constitutionnel* by M. Prêlot (Paris, 1949), p. 447. Cf also, Malberg, *La Loi, expression de la volonté nationale*, Paris 1931, especially pp. 35-45. This masterly work is, also, the driest book I have ever read.

Administrative and judicial decisions are such because they are carried out by agencies whose discretion is fettered by the law under which alone they are empowered to operate. And they too differ from one another in some respects by virtue of their own degrees of discretion. Few laws can be so complete and detailed as not to allow some discretion to the executor or the interpreter. A law condemning all blue-eyed children to death cannot define "blue" without some margin of latitude and this is a "discretion". The Ministry has discretion in that it must decide whether a particular person thing or act falls within the description contained in the law. The role of the Courts is identical in purpose but in fact the Courts have less "discretion" than the administrative bodies because they are bound by a traditional procedure, a body of rules of construction and above all by previous decisions (*stare decisis*) and the administrator is not. He can alter procedures and rules of construction from one case to another and does not need to follow precedents. The difference between Law, Regulation, and Court Decision depends in the first place then, upon the unfettered discretion of the Legislature, the limited discretion of the Departments, and the almost entirely restricted discretion of the Courts.

These three agencies differ from one another sharply in yet another respect—their traditional procedure; that is to say, the technique by which they come to their decision. The decision on Bootle's water rate would be a law if it passed through Parliament with the traditional three readings in each House and then received the assent of the Crown. It would be a rule if made by the Ministry of Health by its traditional form of procedure, and a court decision if arrived at by the Courts with their traditional rules of construction and rules of evidence. This seems to be the sense in which Dicey understood the issue when he commented on the famous case of *Local Government Board versus Arlidge* AC, 120, 84, LJ. KB 72. The problem was: when subject matter formerly handled by the Courts is transferred to a Government Department must the Department also follow the traditional Court procedure? Now—does the subject matter of governmental activity determine the way it must be handled? If so it must follow that when the matter was transferred from Court to the Departments, the latter must copy the Court's traditional way of handling the affair. Dicey in fact, by denying this conclusion, effectively denies the premise:

"When judicial functions" he wrote, "which involve jurisdiction are transferred by Statute from a law court to a government department (e.g. to the Local Government Board) it is possible to entertain one or two opposed views as to the effect of this transfer. The Local Government Board, it may be said on the one hand, is called upon to exercise *judicial functions* or in other words *jurisdiction;* and hence it follows that the Local Government Board must, when acting as a judge, comply with the *rules of judicial procedure* ... On the other hand it may be said that the transference of jurisdiction from a court to the Local Government Board is in itself *prima facie* evidence that Parliament intended that such jurisdiction should be exercised in accordance, not with the *rules which govern judicial procedure*, but with the rules which govern the fair transaction or business by the Local Government Board."[1]

Severely practical conclusions follow from this analysis. Dicey, it is clear, adhered to the view that the nature of the technique employed (which he considered also implied the nature of the agency) determined whether an act was judicial or administrative. The neo-Montesquieu doctrine held in the U.S.A. insists that the actions of government vary by their inherent content and that this content decides whether they fall within the province of Congress, President or the Courts. Consequently the transfer of power, a shift of leadership between the three branches of government has been cramped and thwarted by the tight pigeon-holing of the written Constitution as interpreted by the Supreme Court.[2]

By contrast, the flexibility of the British Constitution has allowed the fullest possible play to the shifting of forces among the three agencies. In the last century the Sovereignty of Parliament and the Rule of Law permitted little discretion to the executive departments. The first operated through minutely detailed statutes and constant Parliamentary enquiry and debate, the second operated by regular judicial review of any executive interpretations of statutes which a private citizen cared to contest. The last half century has seen the discretion of the government departments grow continuously at the expense of the Legislature and the Courts. The first tendency is witnessed by the dominance of the Cabinet over the Commons and its increasing ability to legislate by regulation: the second by the growth of administrative tribunals using administrative methods to deal with matters formerly referred to the Courts.

---

[1] Dicey, *The Development of Administrative Law in England*, LQR, April, 1915.

[2] Cf. P. Herring, *Presidential Leadership*, American Government in Action Series (Farrer and Ringhart, 1940).

CHAPTER 3

THE BRITISH CABINET SYSTEM

"I then spoke at large upon the Constitution of an English Parliament ... ."

Swift: A Voyage to Brobdingnag.

THE sovereign body of Great Britain is the King in Parliament. A hundred years ago, the initiative in law making had passed to one of its constituent members, the House of Commons. To-day this initiative is firmly and incontestably in the hands of what is in fact a kind of steering-committee inside the Commons, namely the Cabinet. But the Cabinet is also directing body of the Executive. The last century has seen the move from Parliamentary to Cabinet Government, in short, the rise of Administrative Leadership. The constitutional role of the Cabinet epitomizes the whole Constitution.

I

The Commons is the energizing element, the mainspring of Parliament. Subject to the qualification introduced by the remaining prerogatives of the Crown and the powers of the Lords as defined in the Parliament Act of 1911, whoever can control the action of the Commons is the effective governing body of the country. The Parliament Act fixes its life at five years. To extend its life—as happened in 1939—necessitates a special law. Normally a general election will take place every five years.

The election campaign is organized by the political parties, and there is a steady tendency in this country for the electorate to be monopolized by two great parties, all others being ground out. This two-party arrangement is not exclusively due to the "inherent common sense" of the British people, though it is tolerable only because of the remarkable national homogeneity of the people of these islands. It is much more immediately due to the one-member

26

constituency and the fact that the candidate at the top of the poll automatically wins the contest, irrespective of whether he has an absolute majority of votes cast. Any third candidate will simply "split the vote" in the constituency. By voting I.L.P. one may defeat the Labour candidate, drawing away a part of his support, benefiting neither the I.L.P. candidate nor the Labour candidate but, paradoxically, the Conservative. The consequences are prodigious. "Floating" voters tend less and less to "throw their votes away" by voting for hopeless "third" candidates, and tend instead to cast their vote for whichever of the two candidates comes nearer their personal point of view. Thus any third party is slowly eliminated, while a party which splits into two and contests the election as *two* factions will lose it. The British electoral system puts a premium on party solidarity.

The election campaign is fought upon the merits of rival party programmes. The assumption is that the victorious party is pledged to carry out its programme, if it succeeds in winning a clear majority of seats in the Commons. It will then claim that this programme has received a popular *mandate*. Because of the two party tendency in England, especially clear-cut at the present moment, the chances of a clear parliamentary majority are almost absolute. Conservatives held undisputed power from 1931 to 1940. The Labour party does so now. The efficient working of the British constitution is premissed on such clear Parliamentary majorities.

Since any Government depends on a consistent majority in the Commons, it must be drawn from members of the majority party. Otherwise it could not long continue. Ministers then, i.e. the heads of government departments, must belong to the majority party. In practice the King, when the election results are known, will send for the known and recognized head of the victorious party and authorize him to "form a government", i.e. to pick the ministers to head the departments of state. These ministers are *not* selected or elected by their party colleagues, whose wishes and predilections do not however go unnoticed. As was said of Mr Attlee's Cabinet of 1945, the selection is based on "age and length of service". The selector is the Prime Minister, and the government is *his* government. If he resigns, the government is broken up. He is like the queen bee— once she leaves the hive, it perishes away. The basis of the government, the group of ministers selected by the King's Prime Minister, is the *Cabinet*, an inner and cohesive group of ministers, with a special constitutional status.

II

The Cabinet enjoys its peculiar authority because its members combine in themselves three kinds of status. It really is three in one and one in three. It is the Executive, because its members are ministers of the Crown, the heads of Government departments, the masters of armies of Civil Servants, nay, of real armies too, and navies and air armadas. But it is also a steering-committee of the Legislature, because its members are also (with one or two minor exceptions) M.P.s. And finally, and most vital, it is a committee of the majority party, for it is composed for the most part of the tried and trusted party chiefs, and in so far as untried party men are given ministerial posts, so they tend to rise in the party hierarchy. The Executive is thus a committee of the Legislature, and enacts by and with its consent, but it gains their consent precisely because it is a party committee and its party controls the Commons! Thus the peculiar dominating role of the Cabinet is a function of *party solidarity*. So long as Cabinet and its party hang together, they will never hang separately. No wonder the French exclaim in wonder!

Surs les murs de Westminster, on voit paraitre ensemble,
Trois pouvoirs étonnes du noeud qui les rassemble.

Astonished at the love-knot which ties 'em all together,
The three powers at Westminster might be knocked
    down with a feather!

The Cabinet is not a mere collection of ministers. It is a corporate unity. This depends on two factors, its collective responsibility and the monolithic nature of its party support.

Each minister is individually responsible to the Commons for the day to day administration of his department. If his policy displeases he may, like Sir Samuel Hoare, have to resign; but the position of the Cabinet is untouched. Many ministers come and go in the life-time of a Parliament while the same essential Cabinet still maintains its supreme position. The corollary of individual ministerial responsibility in England is that the minister declines to have any kind of official committee associated with his administration, whether an "advisory" committee of his own party comrades or a specialized standing committee of the Commons. He alone is responsible: he cannot and does not desire to claim that his decisions are due to the pressure, advice or command of any outside body. If the Commons dislikes those decisions, it may insist on his removal: it may not associate a committee with his work.

Each minister is individually responsible for running his own department but for *policy* the Cabinet is collectively responsible. What is administration and what is policy is for the Cabinet to define. In the famous debate on the Hoare-Laval proposals, the opposition tried to show that the decision had been collectively known and debated, that the whole Cabinet was implicated, and *all* must resign. Mr Baldwin declared the decision was personal to Sir Samuel Hoare and washed the Cabinet's hands of the matter. Nevertheless there *is* a distinction between policy and administration. Mr Ben Smith may be dropped because he mismanages food rationing: that food should be rationed is a *policy* of the Cabinet for which it is collectively responsible. On policy the Cabinet in effect tells the Commons, "You take us and our policy as a whole. You may not pick and choose your policy, approving this, rejecting that. You must take the good with what you think is the bad." The corollary is again, that the Cabinet maintains that it is uniquely responsible and declines to have this responsibility clouded by the behests of any committee, whether the National Executive of the party to which it belongs, or any Committee of the House of Commons.

"Who is responsible for executive current administration, the Government or Parliament? I say it is the Government that is responsible . . . Parliament's business is to check the Government, throw it out if it wants to, go for it, attack it, criticize it by all means, for Parliament is not a body which is organized for current administration—not in this country . . ."[1]

This distinction between policy and administration is vital. It runs through the whole procedure of the House and it illumines the Cabinet's relation to the House. The Second reading of a bill is policy: if the Cabinet are beaten, they must resign. Not so in Committee stage, which deals with the administrative details of the Bill. A Cabinet's financial estimates for the year are policy, and a defeat in them entails its collective resignation. Not so a defeat in

[1] H. Morrison, 3rd Report. Sel. Comm. Proc. Q. 3260.

the Budget: this is taxation, "Ways and Means" of raising money, and if the House does not like one device the Cabinet may substitute another, but will remain in office to do so.

This collective responsibility of the Cabinet for its *policy* itself depends on the monolithic nature of the British political party majority that supports it, just as in France the Cabinet is never *really* a collective unity because of the fluctuating nature of its Parliamentary support.[1] If Cabinets were regularly overthrown by fluctuating combinations of Parliamentary groups, as indeed they were in Great Britain between 1851 and 1868, the Legislature would in effect pick and choose a policy. A Cabinet would be supported for one particular measure, defeated, broken up, modified and reconstituted for another particular measure, and so on. Legislative initiative would prevail and not Executive leadership. Such indeed was the character of French parliamentarism under the Third Republic. The collective responsibility of the Cabinet for a programme decided at the polls depends on its solid party support. This appears to make it the undisputed master of the Commons. American commentators are very prone to regard it as a dictatorship of the Executive, brow-beating and straight-jacketing the Legislature. That is because they stress the disciplinary power of the Cabinet over its own supporters. But they fail to stress the equally important fact that the Cabinet is also the prisoner of its own back benchers.

In many senses certainly, the Cabinet does "control" its party. Too much stress can be laid upon the Cabinet's power to "refuse the whip" to a recalcitrant and rebellious member of the party, thus ensuring that at the next election he will not only not have the support of the local and central party machines but will have to contend *against* them—a formidable obstacle which all but a very few mutineers fail to surmount. Much play is also made with the Prime Minister's power to dissolve, and force a general election. It is very unlikely that any Prime Minister ever need utter such a threat, for it cuts both ways—to face the country as a divided party must inevitably bring the Opposition into power, and the Prime Minister's faction would "control" its rebels only at the cost of its own life. The power to dissolve certainly keeps the party together—but does not necessarily give the front benchers the upper hand. Such control as the Cabinet does exercise is due to less obvious factors. For one thing it creams nearly all the leaders of the party—

[1] A. Soulier, *L'Instabilité Ministérielle sur la IIIième République.*

the back benchers are almost leaderless. Again, the size of modern governments, with Ministers, Under-Secretaries and P.P.S.s[1] is enormous:[2] about 1 in 3 of the present Labour majority is "ministerialist" in one or other of these categories.

The unanimity of Cabinet and majority is dialectical, a give and take. The appearance of "slave driven multitudes" in the lobbies of the House, the "well oiled party machine", "voting-fodder", the "finest brute votes in Europe"—reflects successful stage management. Few revolts ever occur on the floor of the House because the party crises and the necessary compromises occur behind closed doors in the weekly party meetings. The majority is usually content to take the minister's word for it: after all, Cabinet and party are bone of the bone, flesh of the flesh, elected on the same programme, believing in the same things. The party's successes in the future are bound up with the success of its own Cabinet. So all quarrels are lovers' quarrels. But if serious dissension does threaten, both sides are acutely aware of two things—that to show open fissures in the party is only to bring aid and comfort to the opposition,while, in the last resort, to face the country as a divided party is to court complete defeat for both factions. Every English party that has split has always lost the ensuing election—the Tories in 1846, the Liberals in 1886, the Tories in 1906, the Liberals in 1922, the Labour party in 1931.

Because it is collectively responsible to a majority pledged to support it, the modern Cabinet falls heir to the whole constitutional power of the Commons, itself the heir to the constitutional sovereignty of Parliament. Parliament can do everything, "except make a man into a woman and a woman into a man". It is absolutely sovereign: but it is led, cajoled and dominated by the Ministers of the Crown! They wield all executive power. They never need lose a debate nor yield a single point by duress. With a solid party majority, the Cabinet will never be beaten in the House of Commons and can live its five years out in security. And yet this nucleus of vast power must operate democratically. *Because* it is strong, it must be prepared to meet all attacks, to give away damaging information, to

[1] Parliamentary private secretaries. These are non-official posts, strictly speaking, but are increasingly regarded as stepping stones to Ministerial rank.

[2] 18th May, 1949, after 5 P.P.S's had voted against the Government's Ireland Bill, despite a 3-line Whip, Mr Attlee called for their resignation. Thereby he showed that he regarded them as subject to the same rule of collective responsibility as the Cabinet.

court debate, to allow the Opposition to choose its own time and subject of criticism. Nearly half of the Parliamentary session is devoted to courting and sustaining these attacks.

For their part, the Opposition know that they can move tears, but cannot turn a vote. But though they cannot turn a vote, they can turn *voters*. Their criticism is directed outside Parliament, to the electorate, and all debates have in view not the last election but the next one. The people of this country control their government not by the way they voted 'last time' but by the way they may vote 'next time'. Moreover the electorate is an extraordinarily sensitive umpire. The vast mass of voters are convinced Labour or Conservative supporters roughly equal in numbers. It is the "floating vote" which by swinging its support turns one government out and installs its rivals. Now this is only some 3 or 4 per cent of the total electorate, i.e. some 2000 voters in the average constituency. Furthermore, no government knows quite who these people are! It may be the 'housewife', the cyclists or the motorists. Every minority complaint must be wet-nursed.

Consequently every decision of the Cabinet is a calculated risk. Every decision may be challenged, so severely that a new mandate for it becomes necessary. Each one must be considered from a short and long term viewpoint: whether by currying popular favour now the party's position may not be fatally weakened at the next election, or whether by courting unpopularity now one will not prove right in the long run and reap the harvest of victory. The Cabinet is set for five years. Responsibility sits squarely on it alone. But it is daily accountable to the not entirely predictable grievances of a minute section of public support. Prepared for an immediate election, and prepared to court anybody—these maxims of party success condition the leadership and the preponderance of the Cabinet. The collective responsibility of the Cabinet to the Commons presupposes the collective responsibility of its party to the country.

III

Cabinet Government is very suitable for efficient administration. It is *informed*, for the Executive is best in a position to formulate legislation, just as a Legislature is best able to criticize it and amend it.[1] It is *responsible*. No Cabinet with a clear working majority can shuffle off the responsibility for its mistakes. It is *integrated*—the authority of the Ministers is a collegiate one and they must make their policies march together: and this integration is assisted by the doctrine of the party programme and parliamentary mandate. Lastly, it is *accountable*. The Executive and the Legislative can always get down to the crux of the dispute because the Executive is also part and parcel of the Legislative and both continually inform one another. In this context control becomes statesmanlike and relevant. The control itself is all pervasive, by question, by adjournment debates, by "opposition time". If it is true that it never brings a Government down, it is also true that it makes many a government change its mind. And if finally the Government has lost the confidence of the country it is removable: it will not be suffered to continue, as in the U.S.A., at loggerheads with a hostile majority in the House.[2] It is superseded by its rivals: and the democratic process goes on again, *da capo*.

[1] Yet relatively to Parliament the Executive is *too* well-informed. It has in fact, a monopoly of information. This accounts for the surprisingly poor showing of many ex-ministers, once they are in opposition. They are no longer being briefed by the Civil Service. The situation is far worse in Britain than in the U.S.A. where there is no Official Secrets Act. Notwithstanding this, Congress, which takes its role as Legislature seriously, has created in its Legislative Reference Service, its own sources of information, independent of the Executive: while its Legislative Committees enjoy almost unlimited access to departmental information.

[2] To achieve this result, it is not always necessary even to have a general election, as witness the replacement of Mr Chamberlain's Cabinet in 1940 by Mr Churchill's Coalition Cabinet after the Narvik Debate.

BOOK II

THE
CONDITIONS OF ADMINISTRATIVE ORGANIZATION:
FUNCTION

CHAPTER 1

THE STRUCTURE OF THE EXECUTIVE

"... I could see the sides of it, encompassed with several gradations of Galleries and Stairs, at certain intervals, to descend from one to the other ... I could see four or five men running in great haste up the stairs to the top ... and happened rightly to conjecture that they were sent for orders to some person in Authority. ... "

Swift: A Voyage to Laputa.

I

IN all Western democracies the general structure of the Executive is much the same. It is organized with two considerations in view, viz. the *functions* of government, and the *area* served by government. Sometimes[1] the two considerations clash.

Ignoring area for the moment, the Executive is organized on four main principles. There is much too much work for any single all-purpose agency to perform. A parish council can itself perhaps perform all the tasks requisite for its village. Not so the Central Government. The tasks must be broken up into packets and allotted to specialized agencies. This is the division of labour as applied to government and for the same reasons that apply in industry. Thus arise Ministries, Boards and Commissions—"rank on rank, the army of unalterable law". The first principle is thus, *Specialization*.

The seamless web of government is thereby torn to shreds. It must be knit together again. All differentiation calls for increased integration. A task does not become two tasks because it is performed by two people. Synthesis is not, what Professor G. N. Clark once sarcastically called it, "typing the same thing, but twice, on two different typewriters". In the nineteenth century the ministries

[1] See below, pp. 73 *et seq.*

34

were largely autonomous and independent of one another, but so little was being done, and in such distinct fields that this hardly mattered. To-day the range of government activity is so large that it becomes a spectrum of services. Autonomous action is impossible, for each Ministry tends to affect its neighbour's policy. The trend of the twentieth century is towards increasing use of the second principle, which is *Integration*.

Thirdly, because its task is so vast, many agents are needed. Hence the principle of *hierarchy*. Specialization so to speak delegates authority *outwards* from the central source of authority. Hierarchy delegates authority *downwards* from the top. The top, or apex determines and commands, and discretion becomes less and less, mechanical obedience more and more as the pyramid is descended. Thus authority becomes a *Cone*, thus:

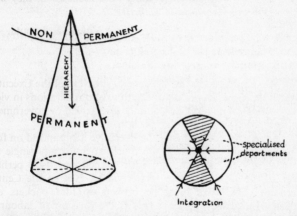

Fourthly comes the principle of *permanency*. The policy makers at the top of the cone of command are the elected agents of the people. They change as popular *will* changes. But the further one moves down the cone of command the less the discretion allowed the agents. At a certain level there is nothing to be gained by turning them out when public will has changed, and much expertness and wisdom to be lost.[1] Below this level, the agents are permanent and

[1] Nothing, that is, except patronage: and there comes a point in an informed democracy where a government loses more because its government is inefficient and costly, then it gains by creating "soft jobs" for its friends.

"politically neutral". The level varies in different countries. In Britain it is drawn far higher up the cone of command than in, say, the U.S.A.

So much for the *functional* consideration and its bearing upon the executive structure. But each of these functions operates within a given geographical area or set of areas. The principles of specialization and integration apply here also but in this context they are better described respectively as *localization* and *centralization*.

It is obvious that one cannot call a Factory Inspector into one's office and tell him to "go out and inspect factories". For practical administration he must be given a prescribed area within which to work. The national area which the government serves must be broken down into sub-areas (field offices, regional H.Q., local government areas). "Localization" is to area what "specialization" is to function.

Then in what relationship must these local areas of administration stand to their central H.Q.? This introduces the second principle, that of *Centralization*. Over whole ranges of function they may be *autonomous* and of equal legal status with the central H.Q. This is the federal relationship, that in which the 48 States of the American Union stand to the Federal authority at Washington. They may be areas which in fact, if not by law, are largely independent of the central ministries, like the English units of local government a century ago. The more rigorous the control exerted over their functions by the central ministries, the more *centralized* is the State. Where all functions are directly administered by the agents of the central ministries, the State is completely unitary, fully centralized. This does not mean that these agents will all operate from the capital city. They may well be commissioned out in sub-districts, to live near their work. These are field stations, and the boundaries of the areas prescribed for them are constructions of the ministry; the stations are without any constitutional life or independence of their own. To set up such field stations is not "decentralization", it is merely to "deconcentrate" centralized power.

One further point is worth noticing here. In decentralized or federal states, where certain functions are performed by elected bodies in the local government or State areas, those elected bodies may be subjected to an identical analysis as this outlined above. They also feel the conflict between specialization and integration. They make use of the principles of permanency and hierarchy. Similarly

36

they also have to consider *area*—and the centralization of Whitehall is paralleled by the centralization of County Councils.[1]

II

The foregoing analysis corresponds to four main levels of administration, viz. a policy-making Cabinet, the Treasury, the departmental and the local or regional.

In England, the Cabinet is the administrative apex and centre, an apex of command, but a centre of functional integration. Though this is a collegiate body, and despite its unitary status, in it each minister ranks equally with his colleagues. Here co-ordination is a product of mutual quarrels, handshakes, glasses of beer and endless compromises; but it is equally the product of three typical devices, viz. the Cabinet Secretariat, the Standing Committees and the recent innovation of "grouped" ministries.

Much necessary integration deals with departmental practices too detailed for the attention of a policy making body, and necessitates also a continuous surveillance such as the Cabinet cannot give. The Treasury is increasingly thrust into the role of co-ordinator at this level.

Such integration could not be achieved however without three presuppositions. The duties of each ministry must be clearly and logically allocated. Their degree of autonomy *vis à vis* the Treasury must be clearly defined. Thirdly, each ministry must itself be unitary, a ministry in fact, not just a collective name covering a dozen or so bickering departments. These ministries must themselves co-ordinate their work, and must co-operate with their neighbours, "interdepartmentally".

Finally, the rendering of day-to-day services to the masses of the State's clients, the enforcement of popular obligations, cannot be performed at Whitehall. Practical administration is a localized matter. "*On gouverne de loin, on administre du près.*" This entails a regional or local level. The service can be performed by the ministry's own agent, installed in the provinces: by the agents of a locally elected authority under the tutelage or control of the Ministry: or by the agents of a locally elected authority in independence of the Ministry.

[1] These matters will be dealt with below, therefore, at Book III, chapters 2, 3 and 4, and for the present attention concentrated on central problems.

CHAPTER 2

THE MINISTRY

"But, how to analyze the Tub was a matter of difficulty . . ."

Swift: A Tale of a Tub.

I

THE vast compass of central government services must somehow
be broken down into manageable portions.

The first question then is the principle on which work should be
allocated, and for this there are four main criteria. Ministries might
be set up to carry out a special purpose or function, such as Health,
or Education in the Ministries with these names. Alternatively it
might look after a special kind of clientèle as for example, the
Children's Department of the Home Office looks after the interests
of all "deprived" children. These are the two primary criteria, but
there are also two others. It is possible to set up ministries according
to the work-process they employ. It is very common, *inside* a ministry, to have a special office of legal advisers, or medical advisers,
or architects or engineers: might it not be possible or desirable to
have a Ministry of Doctors, a Ministry of Lawyers, and a Ministry
of Engineers? Finally, a Ministry may be set up to serve a particular
region. England has many examples—the Scottish Department of
State is one, the Colonial Office another, the India Office, now
defunct, a third.

The first point to notice about these criteria is that they are
not exact. For example: is the Ministry of Agriculture classified
according to its function or according to the agricultural clientèle
it serves? Is the Ministry of Works classified according to its
purpose (Government building) or its works process (for it maintains a great staff of civil engineers). Does the Colonial Office deal
with areas, or with the interests of the Colonial peoples wherever
domiciled?

In the second place, no single criterion is appropriate for all

38

Ministries, nor can any be pushed beyond certain limits. Even Education and Health, the great "functional" Ministries, make concessions to others. Health has to leave some health duties to the Ministry of Labour (factories), the Service Ministries (e.g. the R.A.M.C.), and the Scottish and Colonial Offices. Education likewise "shares" agricultural education with the Ministry of Agriculture, and leaves whole tracts to the Children's Department of the Home Office, to the Services, to the Scottish Department and Colonial Office, even to the Central Office of Information (which is in the Lord President's office). And although the tendency since 1919 is to favour the "functional" kind of Ministry, some branches of government, like the N.A.B.[1] or Children's Department run counter to this trend.

It would be ludicrous to form all departments by the criterion of clientèle. The advantages of such a Ministry are that one authority can perceive all the problems of a special group of people as a single whole, and similarly the members of that group or class need apply to only one single office in any or all of their difficulties. But this criterion is applicable only where the group is so very special that its problems cannot in any way be assimilated to or treated together with those of the nation as a whole. The case against wholesale application of this principle was stated with conclusive force by the Report on the Machinery of Government.[2] "The inevitable outcome of this method of organization is a tendency to Lilliputian administration. It is impossible that the specialized service which each Department has to render to the community can be of as high a standard when its work is at the same time limited to a particular class of persons and extended to every variety of provision for them, as when the Department concentrates itself on the provision of one particular service only by whomsoever required and looks beyond the interests of comparatively small classes."

The "works process" principle could charm only those nations fascinated by the specialist. It is the social religion of all whom Aristotle called the men of one idea. These claim that such an allocation of responsibilities would lead to the highest possible degree of technical specialization, and therefore excellence. The congregated engineers, doctors, lawyers, town planners and educationalists would develop their techniques, and stimulate each other to new heights of discovery and efficiency. This reminds me of

[1] The National Assistance Board.
[2] Cd. 9230 of 1918, § 18.

Thurber, when he says: "Vereker and I stimulated one another—to the point of madness: " even experts have their quarrels. In fact the disadvantages are prodigious. One can ignore the merely ridiculous objections, for example that such a scheme would involve setting up Ministries of Carpentry and Whale Hunting. The vital objection is that such departments call for far more subsequent co-ordination than any other kind to carry a policy through, while making such co-ordination very difficult. No single administrative service could be performed by any single department, and every single department would require the co-operation of a host of mutually antagonistic specialists, each insisting on preferential treatment for their own technical requirements. If merely one single works process failed to fulfil its limited task the whole joint enterprise would be ruined. This is a situation almost perfectly illustrated by the present administration of Housing, where 5 major ministries must all contribute towards the single product.[1]

Finally, as to the regional principle, once again its value is confined to regions so special that their problems cannot be assimilated to those of the nation as a whole. To carry this to its logical conclusion could be to recreate the Heptarchy.

In short, no single criterion is capable of universal application and whichever principle is adopted, some functions must overlap. The form adopted depends upon the problem. If one region has some distinctive character that makes it quite different from the rest, then a separate ministry is justified. Indian health, labour, industrial and educational problems differed in nature from British, simply because they were *Indian*. To have relegated each to the British Ministries of Health, Labour, Education etc., would have lost by dispersion far far more than was gained by specialization. But the same is *not* true of the problems of the County of Kent or the City of Birmingham. Similarly with the "clientèle" principle. Some groups create a distinctive problem. The Red Indians of the U.S.A. do so, and hence a special "Indian Bureau" exists for them. The "deprived children" do so in Britain. Perhaps the best illustration of this point is the fate of the nineteenth century Poor Law Commission. It was in effect a "Ministry of Paupers", even under the name of Local Government Board which it took from 1871 to 1919. A pauper was conceived by the nineteenth century as a special kind of man, pauperism as a special problem, just as a convict is a special kind of man and criminals a

[1] Cf. 8th Rept. Sel. Comm. Estimates Comm. C. Housing Expenditure 1946: also Appx. to 1st Ann. Rept. Min. of Works, 1947.

special problem. So one agency was set up to deal with *all* the matters affecting this special category of Englishmen—their health, education, nutrition, rehabilitation. Not until the twentieth century was there general appreciation of Cobbett's famous remark "What is a pauper? Only a very poor man". With that, the Poor Law was "split up" among the Ministries of Health, Education, Pensions and so forth, i.e. among the functional ministries. As soon as it was recognized that the problems of pauperism were simply problems of general poverty, and the pauper only a poor man, the need for a *special* agency disappeared.

With these qualifications, functional classification offers the best chance of efficiency. More than any other it avoids duplication and overlapping of functions. It encourages the acquisition of special skill and knowledge. It allows one great complex of problems to be studied as a whole. The purpose of such a ministry is clear to the public, its name indicates its responsibilities.[1] Yet it never entirely eliminates overlapping, any more than any filing system or library classification system eliminates cross references. The primary responsibility of one department is very often the secondary responsibility of another. School Health is a secondary interest of the Ministry of Education but the primary interest of the Ministry of Health. Education is a secondary interest of the Ministry of Agriculture, but the primary interest of the Ministry of Education. Sometimes the list reaches formidable proportions. A list of the "principal Government Departments concerned with building and civil engineering work other than housing," contains no less than seventeen![2]

II

What is the best size for a Ministry? Nations differ in their numbers of Ministries. Britain has 32, France 18.

There is no scientific criterion of the ideal size. Some have tried to find one in the so-called "span of control" i.e. the largest number of subordinates with whom a chief can efficiently consult. But experts differ on how great this number really is. Graham Wallas put it as high as 12, Colonel Urwick at 5. The truth is, the number is bound to vary. The individual character of the chief is unpredictable,

[1] Cf. Beveridge Report (Cmd. 6404), para. 44 for an excellent illustration of this principle.

[2] 1st Ann. Rept. Ministry of Works, Cmd. 7279 of 1947, Appx. 1.

and so is that of his subordinates. The character of the administration varies, some offices being "quiet" while others are "lively". Material factors, such as the dispersion of staffs, unsuitable accommodation or office equipment also affect the "span of control".

The large department would appear to have four main advantages. It is more economical than several small ones each with its overheads. The larger it is the more comprehensively can it plan. Thirdly, it achieves co-ordination within this span, because being united under a single chief its various offices can never quarrel so bitterly or so aridly as can several rival ministries each under chiefs of co-equal status: for example the coalescence of Treasury and Ministry of Economics in 1947 eliminated the possibility of rivalry between them. Finally just because the large department co-ordinates over a wider field it reduces the numbers of inter-ministerial boundary disputes, and thereby lightens the work of the policy making body, the Cabinet. These advantages are clearly illustrated in the creation of a Ministry of National Insurance, in 1946. Insurance was administered in an illogical batch of separate and mutually contradictory schemes for various types and classes of persons, with different conditions, eligibilities and rates of benefit Among the advantages of a single Ministry of National Insurance were listed: convenience to the insured person who had one office to deal with, the "avoidance of ... disputes as to which authority is responsible for dealing with a particular case and on what principles;" "the avoidance of overlapping and duplication of benefits;" the avoidance of gaps—the ministry could cover fresh needs as they were recognized without dispute as to which authority was responsible for dealing with them; "uniformity of benefit rates and conditions" and "uniformity of procedure for determination of claims to benefit."[1]

These advantages must, however, be qualified. A ministry cannot be allowed to grow indefinitely large, otherwise there would be no point in having separate ministries at all. The development of English central administration from 1780 is a fascinating history of departments "budding off" from their parents.[2] To take one example, the Poor Law Commission of 1834 was combined in 1871 with certain public health agencies, in 1872 with certain road agencies. As the Local Government Board it developed an interest in housing, local

[1] Bev. Rept. Cmd. 6404, 1942, para. 44.

[2] For the most part from the Secretaries' office (Home Office), and the Privy Council. Cf. Gretton *The King's Government* (Bell, 1913).

government guidance, hospitals, medical insurance. Since 1919 it has lost its road powers to a Ministry of Transport (1919), its town planning powers to the Ministry of Town and Country Planning (1944), its national insurance powers to the Ministry of National Insurance.

The point where further integration becomes harmful is the point at which the task of the Ministry ceases to be a single problem. So long as town planning was a mere question of siting and spacing urban areas it could be associated with the Ministry in charge of housing. As soon as it involved judging between the alternative and rival uses to which land could be put, it began to become a separate problem and required its own ministry. A large department is fictitious when it merely houses a heterogeneous collection of odd offices, like our Home Office, or the Lord President's Office. The only reason for housing these together under a single minister is the advantage of their having a single person to answer for them in Parliament.

"Integration" may become positively harmful, real "Empire building", for it may involve the suppression of some valuable and independent agency. The classical illustration is the Local Government Board. Formed by amalgamation of the old Poor Law commission and the scattered and timorous offices dealing with public health, it was captured from the outset by the poor law personnel who dominated it down to 1919. Its public health activities were suppressed and the pioneer patience of John Simon and Tom Taylor thrown away. Similarly it is argued that so long as the Treasury, which is primarily a Finance ministry, is concerned with staff and establishment questions for the Civil Service as a whole, personnel management will never be treated constructively but always in a penny-pinching and pettifogging way.

This risk, that something valuable may be suppressed by the incorporation of a small independent agency in a large one, will of course be run only where ministries are supposed to speak with one voice and act as a unity. This need not always be so, and where it is not so there seems singularly little point in calling them by a collective name. A Ministry of Social Welfare is not really a Ministry if in fact it consists of several autonomous offices always at war with each other and speaking with a gift of tongues.

Because of their internal organization the U.S.A. and France possess many ministries which *are* purely nominal. The French ministry is composed of "bureaux" the equivalent of our *divisions*.

Each has its chief and all are of equal status. There is no permanent head. His place is taken by a weekly meeting of bureau chiefs.[1] Similarly in the U.S.A. the bureaus of the Departments, under bureau chiefs, very often enjoy an autonomous status to the point where they promote their own legislation in Congress.[2] Only five or six have so-called "Administrative Assistants" the equivalent of our permanent heads.

Britain is in fact looked to as a model of departmental organization. Though the nomenclature differs much from one Ministry to another, the underlying pattern is this. The *whole* Ministry is the responsibility of a single Permanent Head. He is assisted by one or more "Deputy Heads", and between them "blocks" of the Ministry become the particular care of each. But all are also responsible for *general* oversight.

Under this general superintendence are grouped the Divisions (or Departments) of the Ministry, each usually in charge of an *Under Secretary*. (The rank of Principal Assistant Secretary has recently been assimilated to the Under Secretaries). The divisions are sometimes further sub-divided into Branches, each in charge of an Assistant Secretary, who has under him as many offices as necessary each in charge of a Principal and his Assistant Principals.

This organization is hierarchical to a most rigorous degree. It is accused of cumbrousness and lack of flexibility. It is jibed at—the civil servant, it is said never makes a mistake because he sends half of his problems down below him for further information and refers the other half higher up for a decision. But it has the merit of sifting all really controversial questions, so that in the case of conflict between branch and branch, or Division and Division, there is always one single outsider who can and usually does, resolve the dispute.

[1] From 1940-1944, there were created "*Secrétaires-Généraux*", who acted as Permanent Heads. Most have now been discarded.

[2] President's Committee on Admin. Management, 1936, p. 265-7.

CHAPTER 3

THE CABINET

..."*The strong Disposition I observed in them towards news and politics; perpetually enquiring into Public Affairs, giving their judgements in matters of state; and passionately disputing every inch of a party opinion.*

Swift: A Voyage to Laputa.

THE relation of the Cabinet to the party structure and the House of Commons has been discussed already. This chapter is concerned with the operation of the Cabinet as the apex of the Civil Service hierarchy and co-ordinating centre for the departments of Government.

The Cabinet, says Sir Ivor Jennings[1] is the "directing body of the National Policy. Consisting of the principal leaders of the party in power it is able to forward that policy by reason of its control of the House of Commons. Consisting too of the heads of the more important Government departments, it is able to forward its policy by laying down the principles to be followed by the central administrative machine. Their service under the Crown is the legal explanation of the political fact that ministers hold important Government offices. Membership of the Privy Council is a historical survival."

Its functions have been authoritatively defined[2] as:

"(a) The final determination of the policy to be submitted to Parliament;

(b) The supreme control of the national executive in accordance with the policy prescribed by Parliament; and

(c) The continuous co-ordination and delimitation of the functions of the Several Departments of State."

The Cabinet has varied in size throughout the nineteenth and twentieth centuries, the persistent, and indeed, natural tendency, except in times of war (when its membership has been severely pruned back), being towards continuous enlargement. In the

[1] *Cabinet Government*, p. 174.
[2] Rept. of Machinery of Govt. Committee, §6.

nineteenth century it varied between 12 and 15 members. Between the two Great Wars it had risen to 20-21 members. The Attlee Cabinet began in 1945 with 21 members. It has now been cut back to 17. This thrusts a number of ministers outside the Cabinet, for the increase in Ministries has been continuous. To-day there are 15 ministries outside the Cabinet.

The Prime Minister, the Cabinet, and the non-Cabinet ministers were all given statutory recognition by the Ministers of the Crown Act of 1937. What are the relations between them? The Prime Minister is formally both His Majesty's Prime Minister and the First Lord of the Treasury. Theoretically he is a *primus inter pares*. In practice certain incidentals to his position give him a status superior to his colleagues. In the first place it is *his* Cabinet; after receiving the Royal Command *he* picks his colleagues, and if he resigns the whole Cabinet must do so. In addition to this, he is the chief channel of communication with the Crown, he is the leader of his political party, and he usually leads the House of Commons.[1] Even when he does not take up this position (as at present) it is the Prime Minister who is expected to make the more momentous announcements on Government policy, to answer especially grave questions in the House called "Private Notice" questions, and where necessary, to correct statements made by his colleagues which are out of line with Cabinet policy.

The Cabinet ministers are of equal status. But in fact there is bound to be a so-called "Inner Cabinet" of the most powerful men in the party, whose prestige is such as to outsoar the rest. Theoretically, however, all are equal, indeed constitutionally they must be so, for constitutionally each is alone responsible to Parliament for the day to day administration of his department. Such equality of status is the main obstacle in the way of Cabinet unity and gives rise to those suggestions for "grouped ministries" or "super ministers" dealt with below.

The Cabinet Ministers have the right, if it is not indeed an obligation, to attend at every Cabinet meeting, and to receive in full all memoranda and minutes circulated to Cabinet Ministers by the Cabinet Secretariat. In this they are sharply distinguishable from non-Cabinet ministers who are summoned to attend only when their department is under consideration and who receive only those memoranda and extracts from the minutes which affect them and their department. They do not participate in policy making except

[1] From 1945, though Mr Attlee was Prime Minister, Mr Herbert Morrison led the Commons.

in so far as it affects them: but they must support such Cabinet policy or resign. The doctrine of collective responsibility is stretched beyond the Cabinet to the Government.[1]

At first glance it must seem as if government by a committee of equals is the very antithesis of the co-ordinated activity which the modern State demands. The President of the U.S.A., who is constitutionally the chief Executive must, it would appear, co-ordinate far better: he has only his own mind to consult, not 16 bickering colleagues.[2] Furthermore he is, so to speak, in continuous session, unlike the Cabinet which can find time from departmental duties only to meet for 2 hours each week, with a few special meetings from time to time.

This is quite true as far as it goes: the Cabinet must try to approach the unity of a single mind and the self consistency of one individual's memory. To go any further, however, would be to ignore another factor, viz. the burden of the work falling on this "supreme control". Here the Cabinet has a decided advantage over the Presidency. 16 colleagues can divide up and co-operate upon, the work in hand, consult one another in doubt and have the moral support of their colleagues in maintaining their decisions. The U.S. President is overwhelmed with work. He cannot devolve it, for come what may he is in the last resort also constitutionally responsible. "The President needs help!" Such was the verdict of an authoritative American Committee in 1937.[3] In administering the decision of Congress he is alone with his conscience.

The problems of the Cabinet considered as the formulater of policy and the supreme executive thus revolve around three factors. First, here are 16 ambitious, and powerful men, constitutionally of equal status, each with some personal axe to grind, since all or nearly all control a Ministry and are publicly associated with its special line of work. How is a real collective decision to arise? It can do so only through the greatest possible collective *discussion*. How is this achieved? Secondly, the burden of work, both the departmental and Parliamentary duties of the individual ministers, and the mass of decisions which can only be taken at Cabinet level,

[1] And, since Mr Attlee's precedent in May, 1949, even to the P.P.S.'s of ministers. See note to p. 31.
[2] For, in the sense of being the "supreme control of the national executive" it must be stressed, the U.S.A. equivalent of the British Cabinet is *not* the U.S.A. "Cabinet" at all, but the one-man Presidency.
[3] President's Rept. on Administrative Management, 1936.

have multiplied and remultiplied in the last half century.[1] As the Cabinet can occupy itself less and less with details, it only has time for the most general and critical levels of policy. This implies some *sifting* process by which the less important conflicts are settled outside. Thirdly, the very fact that there are 17 minds at work and so 17 impressions of what was decided, together with the mass of work and detail traversed would alone demand some guarantee of self consistency. The infrequent meetings of the Cabinet reinforce this need. A collective memory has become necessary. Collective discussion is attempted through the Committees of the Cabinet. The sifting of matter is secured by the procedure for compiling an Agenda. The collective memory is supplied by the Cabinet Secretariat.

The plenary sessions of the Cabinet act, to a large extent, upon materials already premasticated in Committees. These are of two kinds, the Standing, or Permanent, and the *Ad Hoc*. At the time of writing, there appear to be four Standing Committees. The *Home Affairs Committee* considers the technical aspects of Government bills, i.e. legal and drafting problems and in this it is advised and assisted by the Drafting Office and other officials. It is also responsible for preparing the annual programme of legislation to be included in the King's Speech at the opening of the Session. Its minutes are circulated to the Cabinet and thereafter its recommendations appear on the agenda for final discussion by the whole Cabinet.[2] The *Defence Committee*, formerly the Imperial Defence Committee was reconstituted in 1946 along the lines laid down in the White Paper on the Central Organization for Defence.[3] It consists of the Prime Minister (Chairman) and Minister of Defence (Vice Chairman), the Lord President, the Chancellor of the Exchequer, the three Service Ministers, the Ministers of Labour and Supply, the Foreign Secretary and the 3 chiefs of Staff. This Committee has many sub-committees, e.g. Home Defence, and Overseas Defence. In addition, there are two Economics Committees—(since November 1947) viz. a *General Policy Committee* consisting of the Chancellor and Minister of Economics, the President of the Board of Trade and the Minister of Labour; and a Committee dealing with details, including all the former Ministers, but reinforced by the Ministers of Fuel, Transport and Supply. These new committees replaced two former committees viz. a *Home Economics Committee* and an

[1] See above, p. 15.

[2] Jennings, *Cabinet Government*, p. 199.

[3] Cmd. 6925 of 1946.

Overseas Committee under the Chairmanship of the Lord President and the Prime Minister respectively.

Ad hoc committees, set up to study some particular problem, are far more numerous, and some 30 or so may operate concurrently. They throw a heavy strain upon certain Cabinet Ministers like the Chancellor and the Prime Minister whose presence is, half of the time, indispensable. This is one of the many arguments put forward for an inner cabinet of Ministers-without-portfolio whose prime purpose would be to chair such committees. Generally the committees are small, of not more than two or three interested ministers, but they are reinforced by non-Cabinet Ministers and even civil servants where this is necessary. Generally speaking, an agreed recommendation placed on the Cabinet agenda, will, one can assume, be accepted without further discussion, but it would be perfectly in order for any Cabinet member to challenge it if he wished.

The Committees give interested ministers the chance to bargain and compromise with each other before the Cabinet discusses the matter, and so to make further Cabinet discussion unnecessary. They enable far more work to be accomplished than by mere plenary meetings and these are left clear for discussing just those matters where disagreement is implicit. The "collective responsibility" of the Cabinet thus becomes something of a reality. On the matters agreed by Committees no further collective deliberation is necessary for the interested parties have "got together", and the rest of the Cabinet is prepared to defend their decision. On matters referred to the whole Cabinet for discussion, although there will not necessarily be unanimity, there *is* collective deliberation. This is almost as much unity as can be expected from the inherent nature of Committee Government.

The Committees thus prevent much additional discussion falling on the Cabinet and the way the agenda is compiled tends to prevent some labour from falling upon the Committees. The Committees "sift" Cabinet material, the Agenda sifts Committee material. The present procedure is said[1] to date from the Labour Government of 1924. A departmental memorandum or draft bill must first be circulated to the Treasury, the Law Offices, and any other departments affected.[2] All these are likely to prepare comments or counter

[1] Jennings, *op. cit*. 190.
[2] This procedure was certainly modified during the Second World War. Clearly, Treasury and Law Officers would not receive Foreign Office papers or memos. on strategy in the ordinary course of events: it still remains, by and large, the present practice.

memoranda. This body of documents is then circulated among Cabinet Ministers. At least five days must elapse (unless the Prime Minister waives the condition for some urgent consideration) before the matter finds its way to the Agenda. The memos. are circulated daily, or even more often. The Prime Minister can always, of course, alter the Agenda, or compile an emergency Agenda if the occasion demands. Compare this fairly orderly system with the conditions in the 1906 Cabinet, as described by Lord Haldane one of its members.[1]

"The Cabinet ... was like a meeting of delegates. It consisted of a too large body of members, of whom two or three had the gift of engrossing its attention for their own business. The result of this and the want of system which it produced was that business was not always properly discussed and the general points of view which required clear definition almost never. ..."

The decisions of the full Cabinet, the decision of the sub-committees, the compilation of its agenda, the circulation of its memoranda, are in the hands of the Secretariat. This body was set up only under the pressure of war conditions in 1916. It subsequently proved indispensable, and in the Second Great War it threw out off-shoots in the shape of a Central Statistical Office, and its Economic Section. The institution of a Secretariat worked a truly prodigious change. It is not in any way supra-departmental, it is purely a recording agency, but its co-ordinative effect is revolutionary. For consider the effects upon a fluctuating, busy, short lived committee, meeting for short periods at long intervals of the sheer fact of *records*. In the first place the Cabinet must be clear as to what decision it really did reach: a confused vague sentiment will be queried by the secretary, who will ask, (in effect), "What exactly am I to say Sir?" Contrast this with a situation such as arose in 1903 when Chamberlain quarrelled with, and in effect broke up, the Conservative Cabinet over a disagreement as to what was the exact decision of a former meeting on the matter of Protection. Secondly, this Secretariat is also dispersed to take minutes for the various sub-committees of the Cabinet, so that cross reference to decisions and memos. of other sub-committees is almost automatic. Thirdly, by circulating the memoranda and recommendations to the Cabinet and ensuring that non-Cabinet ministers receive extracts which affect them, it ensures that each member automatically becomes acquainted with the work of the whole, and is briefed as to what he himself is expected to do. Finally, in so far as it preserves

[1] *Autobiography*, pp. 322-23.

these files the Secretariat can point out when and in what form decision on similar or related topics took place. It acts in fact as a *memory*. Just as the memory makes possible the Identity of the Self, so the Secretariat makes possible the self-consistency of the Cabinet, as between the decisions of its component committees, as between one type of decision and another, and as between one meeting and those that succeed it. It is a simple device but its enormous effectiveness is only grasped in its absence.

Despite these techniques and devices, there are not a few ex-Cabinet Ministers who argue forcibly that the Cabinet is still not an efficient body. Mr Amery, for example, accuses ministers of being wrapped up in their departmental duties, interested in Cabinet meetings solely to advance their departmental policies, hastily improvising answers to urgent telegrams. "The one thing that is hardly ever discussed is general policy. ... There are only departmental policies ... the whole system is one of mutual friction and delay with at best some partial measure of mutual adjustment between unrelated policies. It is quite incompatible with any coherent planning of policy as a whole or with the effective execution of such a policy ... ."[1] This appears to be largely true of Mr Attlee's Cabinet also.

The solutions suggested for such a state of affairs consist, in one way or another, of *grouping* ministers together. Sir John Anderson[2] for example, suggests that they be grouped according to their subject matter under Standing Committees of the Cabinet. Mr Amery would go much further; his suggestions are modelled upon the experience of Lloyd George's War Cabinet. He suggests an inner group of six ministers-without-Portfolio, meeting to discuss future policy, and acting as chairmen to the Standing and *ad hoc* Committees. In addition there should be a group of Standing Committees like the Defence Committee each served by its own research and planning staffs drawn from the actual departments themselves. The Prime Minister would be *ex officio* chairman of each, and would appoint his own deputy chairmen. The deputy Chairman would, it seems, not be a "co-ordinator" but a "super minister" in the sense that the Minister of Defence is the recognized policy minister for Defence.

This would involve a drastic remodelling of the Cabinet. The nearest innovation was the creation of the Minister of Defence. He

---

[1] *Thoughts on the Constitution*, p. 87.
[2] *Romanes Lecture*, 1947.

is a Cabinet Minister: the three Service Ministers no longer are. He is responsible for defence policy as a whole, a status marked out by his Deputy Chairmanship of the Defence Committee. In addition, he apportions the respective money, men and material to the three ministries, and settles administrative matters common to the three Services. In fact this is the model which Mr Amery wished to apply to all the Departments, but so far there has been no further extension of this principle. In November 1947 it seemed as if the new Minister of Economics was to play the same role *vis à vis* the Exchequer and production ministries. This was envisaged in Sir Stafford Cripps' chairmanship of the two new Cabinet Standing Committees, and the description of his new role as "co-ordinating" economic affairs. But whereas the Defence Ministers have no right of appeal to the Cabinet except *via* the Defence Minister, the members of the two economic committees have. This solution is far more on Sir John Anderson's pattern—i.e. of Standing Committees—than on Mr Amery's. Nor is this the only example of such a preference. In 1946 a Cabinet Committee was instituted to deal with Housing: it consisted of the ministers concerned and was served by its own special staff, and an interdepartmental committee, called the "H.Q. Building Committee".

There is little doubt that the present Government prefers to let sleeping dogs lie and is disposed to make do and mend with Cabinet Committees and Interdepartmental committees of civil servants. Meanwhile the prodding still goes on, and has even reached official circles. "The necessity ... is for a modification of the present pattern of the administrative machine ... already foreshadowed in the setting up of a single Ministry of Defence to co-ordinate the activities of the three Service Departments.[1] Much influenced by their witness Mr Balliol Scott, himself a former Civil Servant and an "efficiency expert", the Select Committee of Estimates seem to have been impressed by his view that the interdepartmental committee was a mere temporary palliative and that "reform of the machinery at the top" might involve the redistribution of functions between ministries, and the grouping of ministers with related functions under Presiding Ministers.[2] The Labour Government did not seem to favour the suggestion.

[1] Select Comm. Estimates, 1946-7, Sub. Comm. D. 7 Aug., 1947, §48.
[2] *Ibid.*, p. 93.

Chapter 4

TREASURY CONTROL

"... having myself for several months, racked my Invention (if possible) to enrich this Treasury with some additions of my own (which however should have been printed in a different character, that I might not be charged with imposing upon the Publick).

Swift: Polite Conversation.

I

THE Second World War drew attention to the inadequacies of the Cabinet as a co-ordinating agency. It was necessarily preoccupied with high policy. The Departments were engorged with detail. The exigencies of total war created a host of problems common to all the Departments, demanding uniform treatment, but too large for interdepartmental conferences to handle and too petty for the Cabinet. The persistence of economic controls in peace time has accentuated this difficulty. An intermediate authority was needed, "able to appreciate how policy in one sphere may react on others and ... charged with the responsibility for ensuring that the lessons gained from the experience of all the Supply Departments are used to build up the most effective and uniform system ... practicable."[1] In Great Britain there is an authority which does fill this role partially, and which is being pressed further and further to fill it completely. This unique body is one department among the others, viz. the *Treasury*.

The British Treasury is unique in that with its primary function as a Ministry of Finance it combines the control of government personnel, the surveillance of civil service organization and methods, the standardization of certain common procedures and practices, and, to-day, the co-ordination of economic policies. In the U.S.A. the Bureau of the Budget shares these duties with the Treasury, the Civil Service Commission, and the Personnel Liaison Officer of the

[1] 14 Rept. Select. Comm. Nat. Expend. 42-43.

President's Executive Office. In France, the duties are similarly dispersed between the Ministry of Finance, the *Direction de la Fonction Publique* and the Executive Office of the *Président du Conseil*. The Treasury's accretion of powers has its critics in this country but every official investigation has concluded that no practicable alternative exists.[1] The argument is always the same: finance is inextricably meshed with the problems of staff, efficiency and the general economy, and separation would create worse problems than agglomeration.

II

The agency which prepares the Budget tends to become predominant over the other departments. This is inherent in the nature of the Executive Budget. The cardinal principle is Budget *unity*, implying first that one agency and only one reviews the financial programmes of all government departments, and secondly, that these are made comparable by appearing together in *one* document. These were the principles recognized in the 1921 Budget and Accounting Act in the U.S.A. They are still not recognized in France with its Budget, *Budgets Annexes* and *Budgets Extra-ordinaires*. Indeed one may sum up the difference between England and France by saying that whereas the U.K. has one budget in 12 months, the French have 12 budgets in one month.

The significance of Budget unity may be pressed at four levels, each deeper than the one before. At the most shallow level: all that is involved is *review*, itself important for it detects overlapping, it compares expenditures, and remarks novel policies. A deeper level is that of *challenge*. The budget agency may have the right to exact a *justification* for the methods, the organization and the staffing which exact the departments' expenditure, and the new policies which have given rise to it. Thirdly, if the agency may say *no* to such expenditure, without appeal, this is the level of *control*. It is a step—but a very large one—from such negative *control* to positive *direction*. The budget agency becomes pre-eminent therefore to the degree that it may say "no" without appeal. The very nature of its task puts it in the heart of things. Finance is needed for every act of administration, hence it reviews all activities of government, while *wise* spending implies a review of staff, organization and methods.

[1] 14th Report p. 31; 16th Report, 1942; 5th Report Select Comm. Estimates, §41.

Furthermore, national expenditure running at nearly one-third of the national income, is now the largest single constituent of national economic policy. The control of finance is central to all government activity and organization.

Budgetary control may of course be watered down by the action of the Legislature. The executive which prepares the Budget is only the instrument of the Legislature and its Budget is only a proposal. There are three major ways where the Legislature's legitimate interests may hinder the executive's integration of the departments through budgetary means. In the first place, the Legislature has the right and duty to satisfy itself that the policies are sound. This may enable a Ministry to appeal to it over the head of the budget agency. The practice is commonplace in the U.S.A., unheard of in Britain where Standing Orders lay it down that proposals for Government expenditure may emanate only from the government, where Parliament may only move the reduction of votes, and where these are always taken by the Government to be questions of confidence. Secondly it has the right and duty of seeing that sums are administered economically and hence to investigate methods and organization. This role is played in Britain by the Public Accounts Committee and the Select Committee of Estimates but it is attenuated and intermittent compared with the standing committees of the American Congress and French National Assembly.[1] Finally the Legislature must insist that the sums are spent as voted. This involves the "Laundry-book" sort of accounts whereas economic planning demands accounts similar to those of a private firm, i.e. the kind involved in the "Budget White Papers".[2] The British practice is now to prepare and debate both kinds. In Britain the Executive's Estimates are voted as proposed; the departments have little or no appeal from the Treasury to the Parliament. There is only an appeal to the Cabinet. Failing that the Treasury has the last word.

III

Until February 1948, the Treasury was organized in three main divisions dealing with Finance, Supply, and Machinery of Government. Since then a new parliamentary under-Secretary has been

[1] Cf. Minutes of Evidence 3rd Rept. Select Comm. Procedure, 1947, p. 113.

[2] Cf. J. R. Hicks *The Problem of Budgetary Reform*, Oxford, 1948.

appointed to deal with Economic matters, and this has added certain units to the Treasury: these are organized as a separate division.

Financial control affects the Finance and the Establishment and Supply Divisions only. The Finance division contains an "Estimates Clerk", who gives final expression to the "Treasury control" of Estimates. The Supply and Establishment division with the exception of Establishments (General) and Organization and Methods Divisions *parallel* the other ministries.

Through control of the *Estimates*, the Treasury exercises a sort of pre-natal (some would suggest contraceptive!) control over departmental policy; through its concurrent control of departmental spending it makes sure that departments spend in strict conformity with the Parliamentary Votes; the information it thereby receives gives it an essential understanding of what the departments are doing. The post-audit carried out by the Comptroller and Auditor General for the Public Accounts Committee necessarily involves the Treasury: it is designed to make sure that ministries have spent money only as charged by Parliament. The last two functions do not primarily affect the question as to how the Treasury controls departmental *policy*, because it is "control" only in the sense that it ensures that Departments spend according to the Estimates they drew up and presented to Parliament, and for which sanction was given. It merely prevents them from being arbitrary. If by control is meant a control over *policy*, this is not where to find it. Is it to be found in the Treasury's authority over *Estimates*?

The Civil Estimates are prepared and presented by the Treasury. The Defence Estimates are prepared and presented by the Service Departments. To-day the distinction is formal.

Each October the Treasury circularizes the Departments with 3 documents, a "caveat" that last year's expenditure is not to be taken as a base line, an Estimate form in which last year's figures are printed in one column, the other being left blank, and a form of explanation to be used in explaining any changes in any individual sub-heads. Where the last does not apply, the Department supplies the Treasury with a general covering explanation. The Departmental Estimate arrives in the Estimates Division of the Financial Division of the Treasury where a junior notes all increases and decreases either in staff or supply. They are compared with the record of Treasury sanctions made during the last year under its "concurrent audit powers". They will have been sanctioned by the

THE TREASURY

PERMANENT SECRETARY

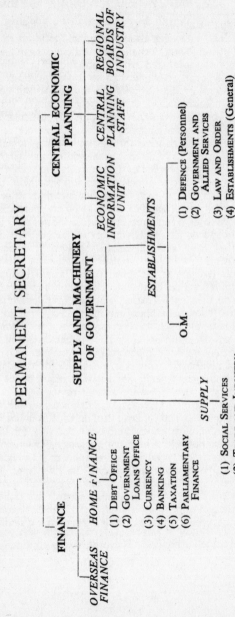

FINANCE

OVERSEAS FINANCE

HOME FINANCE

(1) Debt Office
(2) Government Loans Office
(3) Currency
(4) Banking
(5) Taxation
(6) Parliamentary Finance

SUPPLY AND MACHINERY OF GOVERNMENT

SUPPLY

(1) Social Services
(2) Trade and Industry
(3) Imperial and Foreign
(4) Defence (Policy and Material)

ESTABLISHMENTS

O.M.

(1) Defence (Personnel)
(2) Government and Allied Services
(3) Law and Order
(4) Establishments (General)

CENTRAL ECONOMIC PLANNING

ECONOMIC INFORMATION UNIT

CENTRAL PLANNING STAFF

REGIONAL BOARDS OF INDUSTRY

Supply and Establishment Divisions which parallel the government departments, and which always refer their decisions to the Finance side for record. Thus all changes should either have had a previous sanction, or be accounted for by explanation. The Estimate Clerk is faced by the unexpected effects of sanctions previously given by the Treasury, and by the effects of new proposals. But he is a purely financial officer and so on these matters he consults the Supply and Establishment division which deals with this particular department. The staff of that division are specialists in the work of the Department to which it is assigned, through long dealings together, through the revealing details of its concurrent audit, and often because they have at some time worked in the ministries which they superintend. There follows a period of negotiation and wrangling. The Estimate is finally shot back to the Finance side and finds its way up to the Financial Secretary. He directs action on any points submitted by his subordinates. Then he must consider the general bearing of the Estimate and decide finally whether to submit, refer or amend it. In the last case, failing agreement between Permanent Heads of Departments it will "go to Ministers". In the last resort, the appeal from the Treasury is a Cabinet matter and Treasury control of Estimates reflects the Chancellor's importance in the Cabinet.

How far then is the Treasury's powers over departmental finance a "control"? Any department may fight a decision up to the Cabinet. Furthermore, although the Treasury can say "*no*", it does not seek to tell the Departments how they ought to spend, or what—the department's autonomy in policy making may be hampered, but it is not abolished. Again, the great bulk of spending is to-day largely determined by *policy*, and Parliamentary policy at that: you cannot have a Health Service without paying for it. This confines Treasury "control" to screwing the Estimates down: but there the Treasury must also take a great deal on trust. It is not in a position to check unit costs except in special and very limited cases; it certainly cannot tell a Ministry what, say, Educational policy or Foreign policy or Naval policy ought to be. (Though it may cut nearer the bone when dealing with the Economic Ministries—a fact reflected in its absorption of the Ministry of Economics.) To use the terms with which this section started, the Treasury reviews and challenges rather than *controls*: and in these financial respects, at any rate, even if in some cases it *does* control, it cannot be said to *direct*.

IV

"Control" over Estimates does not however exhaust the Treasury's influence on departmental policy. This is due to the administrative implications of Estimates. They are at once a *wider* aspect of staffing, contracting, organization and methods, and also a narrow aspect of general economic policy. The path to a special and superior status for the Treasury is marked first by its interest in staff questions, more recently by its interest in personnel organization, and finally by its direction of economic policy. It is a journey which began in 1850 when Sir Charles Trevelyan, (himself the permanent head of the Treasury) suggested that it should watch the departments as "a master manufacturer watches his machinery";[1] and since then every step in this direction has been strenuously resisted not only by the Departments, but, paradoxically by the Treasury itself! The departments have not unnaturally clung to their autonomy: and the Treasury has refused to shoulder "their" responsibilities. "Of all the witnesses who have been heard *none* has emphasized the importance of maintaining the doctrine of departmental responsibility more strongly than the representatives of the Treasury itself."[2] Nevertheless, it has been forced far along this road.

The Treasury's interest in staffing springs naturally from its interest in Estimates. A very large part of the Estimates are wage bills,[3] indeed in some ministries such as the Home Office, almost the whole Estimate consists of salaries. Again, as paymaster to this vast force of civil servants the Treasury must take the predominant interest in their classification and scales of salaries, as well as in their numbers. This has always proved the decisive factor in arguing whether the seat of personnel control should not be separated from the Treasury and transferred elsewhere (as in France and the U.S.A.[4]). Its control over staffing derives in the first instance, then, from its control over expenditure. Any proposed increase on authorized establishments must receive the Treasury's approval, and, before approving, it must satisfy itself that the appointment is necessary.

[1] Papers relating to the Reorganization of the Civil Service, 1855. *Memorandum on some branches of the Business of the Treasury* by C. Trevelyan.

[2] 16th Report. Nat. Expend., 1942, §69.

[3] The wage bill of central government was £592 millions, 1947.

[4] Cf. 16th Report. *ibidem*, paras. 95-102.

This is no more a limitation of departmental autonomy than is "control" over any other expenditure. But the Treasury also has a more direct interest derived from the Order in Council of 1920. By Section 6 of Order 1976, the Treasury

"may make regulations for controlling the conduct of H.M. Civil Establishments and providing for the classification, remuneration and other conditions of service of all persons employed therein whether permanently or temporarily."

Furthermore, under Section 4, the regulations regarding entry (which are made by the Civil Service Commissioners) must be approved by the Treasury. This Order is the outcome of a century of pressure upon the Treasury to involve itself in staff matters. It began with the introduction of limited competition in 1855 and developed through a maze of Royal Commissions down to the First World War.

Now the purpose of such pressure was always to get the Treasury to set up some special office or division devoted to Establishment questions. The MacDonnell Commission (1912) wanted: "a special section for the general supervision and control of the Civil Service", the Haldane Committee (1918) demanded a "separate branch specializing in establishment work", the Bradbury Committee (1919) the erection of an Establishments Division. The present machinery was evolved in answer to this pressure but it carefully maintained the autonomy of the Departments. It assigned to the Treasury a status as co-ordinator, and indeed the director of general questions of pay, classification etc.—but beyond that, the discipline, promotion, and deployment of the departmental staffs remained uniquely the responsibility of the Minister. The machinery curiously resembles that of financial accounting. Just as each department of any size has its Finance Officer (the Permanent Head) responsible to the C.A.G.[1] and Treasury for his appropriation accounts, so the larger departments have each an Establishment Officer, directly responsible to the Permanent Head, and exercising by delegation the Minister's control over the staff. He forms the link between the department and the Treasury in so far as all establishment matters are concerned.

Beyond this arrangement the Treasury was simply not prepared to go. Deferring to pressure, they did in 1919 create a separate Division dealing with Establishments, only to amalgamate it with

[1] The Comptroller and Auditor-General.

Supply some eight years later. They declined to repeat the experiment in 1942 notwithstanding the recommendations of the Committee of National Expenditure.[1] Above all they soft-pedalled the proposals, made ever since 1912, that they should set up a branch to supervise the deployment of personnel within the departments.[2] Their response was, we are authoritatively told, "meagre in the extreme". Four officers, known as Investigating Officers were established in 1919. Their task soon became almost entirely confined to advising on office machinery and mechanical appliances. The Second World War provoked a new wave of pressure and this time led to the creation of the Organization and Methods division. (O.M.). There was a further risk of interfering with departmental autonomy.

Now a control over "organization and methods", i.e. the deployment and efficient use of personnel represents much more intimate control of departments than the negotiation of the pay, classifiaction and number of their staffs. In the words of the Committee of National Expenditure, "this development is a clear example of interference with departmental independence."[3] "Nevertheless," continued the Committee, "it is a form of interference which is wholly beneficial. Indeed your Committee's main criticism of the developments which followed the initiative taken by the Treasury is that they have not been carried *far enough*. After some unhappy experiences during the War Years in which at least one of its teams was "bundled out"[4] of a Department, the Treasury was prodded into making some show of response. In 1947 the Committee of Estimates reported on the O.M. division and its effect on the Government departments.[5] The Treasury had once again dug out its well worn compromise for the larger departments have set up their *own* O.M. Branches. Their status varies considerably. Some Departmental Heads (e.g. in the new M.N.I.)[6] clearly believe in them. Others give one the impression of paying a weary lip service to the Committee's devotion to the " 'O.M.' concept." To read their evidence is to understand Mr Dale's[7] description of the

[1] 16th Report, Select Committee of National Expenditure, para. 104.

[2] For the proposals cf. *op. cit.* pp. 15-18.

[3] *Op. cit.* §76.

[4] *Op. cit.* p. 18.

[5] 5th Report, Sub-Committee D, Select Committee of Estimates, 1947.

[6] The Ministry of National Insurance.

[7] Dale's *The Higher Civil Service*.

Civil Servants' attitude as "Stoic realism". The Treasury did indeed set up its own O.M. division, but its duties were to make *general* investigations. Specific investigations and services were to be carried out only for departments having no O.M. branch of their own.

The Treasury then, remained once again master of the field. The so-called "clear ... interference with departmental independence" of 1942 gave way to the 1947 opinion[1] that "there was no evidence that the departmental O.M. branches regarded the Treasury O.M. Division as being associated with the Treasury role of financial policeman": and the division of functions which had come about was expressly commended. It shows once again a striking parallel to Accounting and Establishments.

IV

Thus the Treasury may be the "Department of Departments", but its control of policy is limited and never amounts to direction. And indeed, although it has power, it acts by influence. Its real strength lies in the fact that it is represented on every important interdepartmental committee: that it tends to get the pick of the Civil Service and so strongly influence these committees: and that, since its Permanent Head is the Prime Minister's adviser on all top-flight appointments, it can move the Civil Service towards a coherence of policy by seeing that most senior officials think alike.

Almost in amazement, the Committee of National Expenditure in 1943 discovered the limited nature of "Treasury control". "It is commonly assumed," they wrote, "that the Treasury exert a close and detailed supervisory control over the way in which the expenditure of the Supply Departments is incurred. This assumption goes too far. The function of the Treasury, which is primarily one of sanctioning the undertaking of new expenditure is—so far as concerns the terms on which goods are purchased and contract prices are settled—rather one of co-ordination than control; and while the Treasury are generally concerned to ensure that government business is conducted on sound principles their representatives have emphasized that they 'regard it as important to maintain the position that the responsibility for each individual contract rests

[1] Sel. Comm. Estimates, 5th Report, 1947; §41.

with the Minister for the Department concerned.' "[1] Again the magic formula! They investigated in despair the jungle of departmental procedures and practices in negotiating contracts, and the inadequacy of the Contracts Co-ordinating Committee of the Treasury. The most they could squeeze from the Treasury was a change in the status of Chairman.[2] They could not shake it from its faith in interdepartmental committees. In the view of the Committee nothing would suffice but the "creation of a supra departmental authority to be responsible for the general plan of war production and thus to ensure the proper allocation of resources." Furthermore no other department could play this part but the Treasury.[3] The Treasury replied, tartly, that the divergencies in departmental practices were "impossible to foresee, difficult to detect during their growth and untractable in their solution when practices have crystallized."[4] To "check the actual working of these systems or to undertake any part of the Department's responsibility for ensuring the maintenance and improvement of efficiency in production" seemed to them "an unwarrantable interference".[5]

The truth which lies at the back of Treasury reluctance is surely that one department—and the Treasury is a department—cannot *direct* the policy of any other *unless* the Minister responsible is constitutionally empowered to give directions to another Minister! In short all efforts to turn the Treasury into a super department will and must fail unless the Cabinet is reorganized on the pattern of the Defence Ministry's relationship with the three Services. It is this that gives poignancy to the new situation of the Treasury since the Ministry of Economics was amalgamated with it. For the Minister of Economics was to "co-ordinate" the Production ministries, a position recognized in his chairmanship of the two Economic Committees of the Cabinet. He had the role of "co-ordination of the economic policy of the Government".[6] What degree of direction was thereby entailed? The Ministry of Economics had hardly begun to function before its amalgamation. The Economic Planning Staff never fulfilled its original purpose as the economic counterpart of the Chiefs of Staffs Committee and their joint planning committees. The formal relationship of the "new" Treasury to the economic ministries has hardly arisen, since to a large extent it can be assumed to depend at the moment on the personal primacy of Sir Stafford

[1] 14th Rept. Comm. Nat. Expend., §14.   [2] *Ibid.*, p. 11.
[3] *Ibid.*, pp. 30-31.   [4] *Ibid.*, p. 31, §67.   [5] *Ibid.*, p. 11, § 19.
[6] Hansard, 2 Feb. 1948, 1472.

Cripps[1] among the relatively young and new men heading those ministries. Given a change of personalities and the new status of the Treasury must somehow be formalized. Meanwhile one must assume its role to continue as the department of departments, reviewing and challenging estimates, regulating interdepartmental staff policy, co-ordinating O.M., contracts, regional boundaries, and now presumably economic policies—but directing, never.

[1] Since this chapter was written Mr Francis Williams's book *Triple Challenge* was published. Chapter 5, on the Cabinet, describes how this personal relationship has developed.

CHAPTER 5

CO-OPERATION BETWEEN DEPARTMENTS

"In these colleges the Professors contrive new Rules and Methods of Agriculture and Building, and new instruments and tools for all trades whereby as they undertake, one man shall do the work of Ten: A Palace may be built in a Week, of materials so durable as to last for ever without repairing. ... The only inconvenience is that none of these projects are brought to Perfection: and in the meantime the whole country lies miserably waste, the Houses in ruins and the people without food and clothes. By all which instead of being discouraged they are fifty times more violently bent upon prosecuting their schemes. ..."

Swift: A Voyage to Laputa.

"The minds of these People are so taken up with intense speculations that they neither can speak or attend to the discourse of others without being roused by some external taction upon the organs of Speech and Hearing. ..."

Swift: A Voyage to Laputa.

THE distinction between Policy and Administration, between Plan and Execution, at best a highly theoretical one, is quite blurred in practice. The Cabinet ought in theory to confine itself to plans, leaving the Departments to mere execution. This is not necessarily *good* theory: and it is certainly not current practice. In fact the Cabinet acts largely as a court of appeal settling inter-departmental disputes. This argues a lack of co-ordinating machinery lower down in the hierarchy. The Treasury interposes itself as a sort of buffer between the disputing departments and the Cabinet, and so faces two ways. Some of its work, viz. the review and challenge of Estimates, and the handling of personnel problems, is concerned with policy. In so far as its preponderant influence settles these matters, it relieves the Cabinet of much "sub"-policy making. Other aspects of its work—for example its Chairmanship of the Contracts Co-ordinating Committee, or the Committee on Regional

C   65

Organization—are incidents to mere execution, and here, it declines to do more than act as "honest broker".

The real body of friction and dispute occurs in the actual execution of policy, i.e. at the departmental level. This is inevitable. The more detailed matters become the greater the chances of friction. And detail is the essence of execution as general principle is the essence of policy.[1] Friction must occur because no means of classifying the work of departments makes them entirely self contained,[2] the primary interest of the one being the secondary interest of another. Hence a triple need for co-ordination. Two (or even more) departments may claim exclusive jurisdiction over a given matter. The Fleet Air Arm was for a long time a bone of contention between Admiralty and R.A.F., the control of child health between the Local Government Board and the Board of Education. Or both departments may decline jurisdiction. This in common practice is known as "passing the buck".[3] Finally, both departments may have a legitimate interest in a single matter but give contradictory decisions. Thus the Ministries of Planning, Transport, Agriculture, Health and many others may have a legitimate interest in the site of a health clinic and issue different instructions on the matter. This is the most important class by far.

Similarly in the field of supplies and services. Usually their control or purchase is confined to a single ministry, which acts on behalf of all the others.[4] But two or more may *compete* for limited supplies and force the price up—a very common practice during the Second World War and which the Ministry of Production was finally organized to limit. Similarly two departments may both have a legitimate interest in the purchase or control but go about this in quite different ways. Five departments investigated in 1940 each adopted dissimilar methods of contracting for war supplies.[5]

Lastly, friction may arise from the consequences of our having adopted a primarily functional classification for our departments. One department must consequently act on behalf of another. To build a house five major departments have to collaborate. The Town and Country Planning Ministry clear sites for the rest of the Departments, the Board of Trade controls certain raw materials for

[1] Cf. Book I, Chapter 2.
[2] See above, Book II, Chapter 2.
[3] It needs no further comment.
[4] Cf. 4th Rept. Comm. Nat. Expenditure, 1940 "Contracts".
[5] *Ibid.*, paras. 77-84.

the rest of the Departments, the Ministry of Labour tries to provide for their labour requirements, the Ministry of Works controls licences for them: and the Ministry of Health, "responsible" for housing, must secure some services from each one.

Now these kinds of matters are *not* the Treasury's affair: each affects too limited a number of ministries and too specific an object for the Treasury to undertake the co-ordination. *A fortiori*, they are not Cabinet matters. They arise in the simple execution of departmental policy, from the fact that there can be no perfect classification of departmental functions.

Periodical re-allocation of duties between the various Ministries could certainly prevent a great many disputes. To suggest such a re-allocation was the primary task of the Haldane Committee of 1918 which proposed ten Departments. From the days of Sir Charles Trevelyan a century ago, it has been suggested also that some *permanent* body should be erected at Cabinet and Treasury level to keep watch on departmental activities and re-allocate them[1]. The demand was made again in 1947, by the Select Committee on Estimates.[2] Mr Balliol Scott, formerly employed by the O.M. branch of the Treasury stated the case in its most uncompromising form. "If the machinery of Government were blue-printed the resulting organization structure of the Civil Service would be seen to have many defects in design ... the machine should be so re-designed that the responsibility for taking any decision ... even one involving several departments, lies in one place only."[3] Sir Edward Bridges, the Permanent Head of the Treasury was considerably more restrained. He thought the overlapping more apparent than real; that re-arrangement was never perfect and only produced equally awkward points of division elsewhere; that reform of structure generally resulted from political changes which demanded that a certain question be handled in a different way. "I think," he concluded, "the re-allocations of functions between departments are apt to be made *ad hoc* and on particular occasions, rather than as a result of a comprehensive scheme. Looked at in retrospect, I think you can see a pattern in these re-allocations but I do not think you

---

[1] Haldane Committee Report, 1918; Tomlin Commission, Cmd. 3909 of 1932, para 594; Committee of National Expenditure especially 16th Report 1942, paras. 85-87 and 116; 14th Report 1943, para. 68.

[2] 5th Report, "O. & M." 1947, paras. 47-49.

[3] *Loc. cit.* p. 93.

will get them all worked out and applied at the same time."[1] The chasm between his view and Balliol Scott is not narrower than that between Edmund Burke and Tom Paine. With this view the Committee had to content itself, but not until Sir Edward revealed the existence of a Cabinet Committee on the Machinery of Government, and the formation of an interdepartmental committee on Civil Service efficiency, consisting of Departmental Heads with himself in the Chair.[2]

The situation thus remains unchanged. Nevertheless administration goes on despite occasional absurdities and rather less occasional delays. On the whole things find their proper places, despite the multiple possibilities of friction and misunderstandings between ministries. How in the absence of Mr Balliol Scott do the departments in fact manage to co-operate?

The most important unifying element in the British administrative structure is not formal at all. It is the habit of mind of the Administrative Grade of civil servants. Mr Dale's delightful work *The Higher Civil Service* creates its atmosphere incomparably. The Civil Service is imbued with (in Sir Ernest's Barker's phrase) a "tradition of Civility". The Administrative Grade is drawn from a wider spread of social classes than ever before, yet still comes to a major extent from the two older universities, the essence of whose purpose it is to educate in this tradition. The nature of recruitment, by a *general* examination, provides a common background of the humanities. The slow turnover among civil servants injects recruits into the service in small doses so that they become absorbed into its tradition which they are not numerous enough themselves to disturb. The change from hatless and shambling undergraduate into a close-cropped, black bowler-hatted man about town, is almost instantaneous. They come to use the same half dozen clubs that ring Whitehall, and so regularly meet one another informally. Thus, for example, the Reform Club at lunch time after some much publicized government decision produces a sort of "feeling of the House" among the civil servants who frequent it. The Administrative Grade—it is not large in number, only three or four thousand—forms probably the most homogeneous corporation in the British Isles. The long term cumulative effect of informal collaboration—ringing up, chatting at lunch, "dropping in to see" is prodigious. Least visible publicly, it is the most powerful cement in the whole

[1] 5th Report, Select Committee of Estimates, 1947, Q. 1631-1634.
[2] *Ibid.* Q. 1624.

executive structure. Of course there are always "opposite numbers" whom one cannot abide, "sticky" persons, obstinate persons and stupid persons. No club is free of them. But one has only to compare the British administrative class with its French and American counterparts to see the beneficial results of the British recruiting system, as against a technical and specialized recruitment by each individual ministry as in France,[1] or the constant ebb and flow of civil servants to and from private industry as in the U.S.A.[2]

Nevertheless formal methods of collaboration are essential. One predominant kind flows from the functional character of most British ministries. The Ministry of Health operates the School Medical Service on behalf of the Ministry of Education. Its Chief Medical Officer is also the Chief Medical Officer of the Ministry of Education. The Ministry of Health also organizes medical benefits on behalf of the Ministry of National Insurance, the National Assistance Board pay out unemployment benefits for it at the Labour Exchanges, and the Ministry of Works builds for it.

Another common device is a standing joint Advisory Committee. A good example is the Central Advisory Water Committee on which the Scottish Department, the Ministries of Health and of Agriculture are all represented. The Committee reports to the Cabinet, i.e. it is genuinely supra-departmental. The same three ministries are represented on the Joint Advisory Council of River and Streams Pollution. Health is again represented on the Ministry of Transport's Advisory Council on Street Lighting.

Most common of all however is the interdepartmental committee or conference. The whole Administrative grade is a network of criss-crossing and ephemeral committees arising out of the very course of execution, disappearing and reappearing as the situation demands. Few are erected by any formal process. They are thrown up mostly by the spontaneous initiative of the civil servant. They represent the way civil servants actually carry out a decision. It is generally assumed that all they do is to telephone or dictate orders to their typists, then pass on to the next file—or a round of golf. Not at all. One cannot do better than quote from Sir Oliver Franks's *Experience of a University Teacher in the Civil Service*.[3] He stresses the "reality and extent of delegation"[4]. Unless a junior asked for

---

[1] Up to 1945. Since then their Civil Service has been remodelled.

[2] Cf., President's Committee on Recruitment of Civil Service, 1941 (U.S.A.).

[3] O.U.P. 1947.   [4] *Ibid.* p. 12.

help he was assumed to be coping with his work, and was left alone to carry it out in his own way. How did he do so? "Every official ... had to take some executive responsibility for the policies he devised or received from his superiors. Once he was clear about what in general was desirable he would normally go on to find out, through inquiry, consultations and meetings with experts, what was practicable in the circumstances, establishing the main heads of a workable scheme and identifying the agents whether members of the Civil Service or of the public who must carry out the several parts of the scheme He would then cal a meeting of all these people, and go through the plans, explaining the policy and the steps worked out to realize it, to make sure that each main agent knew his part and its general context and was convinced that his part and the whole scheme was practicable. Having thus established agreement based on understanding he would give word to start operations ... even so he would arrange for progress reports so that difficulties or delays could be ascertained and dealt with before they grew to proportions which would wreck the scheme or its timing and relevance to wider plans."[1]

It may be wondered, what is the incentive to do all this? The answer is really much simpler than it looks, as anybody in the Services or Administration can say—one simply doesn't want or care to bother one's superiors. Constantly to do so is self-depreciation. Most people's general reaction is precisely—"leave me alone —I can deal with this": the civil servant is no exception. His superiors are busy, so why worry them, particularly when ability to get things done without assistance is a first qualification for promotion. Assistant Principals collaborate so as not to bother their Principals, the Principals so as not to bother their Assistant-Secretaries and so on up to the Permanent Heads whose cardinal principle is not to bother the Ministers. This point comes out clearly in a description of the Building Materials Committee. "The supplies," said a witness,[2] "tend, generally to be a little less than the estimates and the job of the Materials Committee is—by inter-departmental consultation and if necessary decision over the head of any department—to settle the division of the available supplies of timber among the various users. ... Q. Do the proposals go before the Cabinet, or is there some small committee consisting of the

[1] *Ibid.*, p. 12.

[2] Select Comm. Estimates Sub.-Com. C. (Housing Expenditure), 1945-6, Qq. 518-520.

particular ministers concerned?—I think one may say that in the light of what is now long experience, the Committee manages not to disagree ... the whole system is based upon securing agreement because everybody knows that they have got to work within the framework."

The interdepartmental committee is ubiquitous.[1] Housing policy is centrally controlled by an interdepartmental committee, the H.Q. Building Committee.[2] The Distribution of Industry is controlled by the so-called "Panel A" another interdepartmental committee. The Ministry of Labour alone is represented on the Standing Committee on Rehabilitation and Resettlement of Disabled Persons, the Schedule of Reserved Occupations Committee, the Preference Sub-Committee of the Labour Co-ordinating Committee, the Distribution of Industry Panels A and B, the Committee for the Employment of supplementary Labour. The story is told of a Foreign Office official who was detailed to do nothing but to make the round of the committees the Office was represented upon, and spent his afternoons looking in, smoking a pipe, and catching his taxi to the next committee. As the European war ended an *ad hoc* committee was summoned calling itself "Committee on the Spontaneous Manifestation of Personal Gratification on the Cessation of Hostilities". A sceptical smile does not at all shake my informant who insists that the committee not only sat but took itself very seriously.[3]

The Interdepartmental Committee has grave limitations, of course. Much depends on their voting procedure.[4] D.I. Panels and Regional Building Committees seem to be able to work rapidly and to refer little to H.Q.: they have perfected a majority vote procedure. Nevertheless, such procedures must always be subject to the *Liberum Veto* of any representative. In the last resort he can always take the matter up to his superiors, or have it "referred to Ministers". The principle of Ministerial responsibility imposes this condition even at this level: it is mitigated by the desire, mentioned above to accept any reasonable compromise rather than worry the Minister. Other reasons why such committees break down are those inherent in any

[1] *Ibid.*, pp. 3-4, 5; 54-5.

[2] 1st Report, Ministry of Works, 1947, p. 9.

[3] Another colleague with extensive experience in the war-time Civil Service, is less sceptical. His enthusiastic comment on this passage runs: "I am inclined to bet this was a Home Office Committee! The literary style is theirs."

[4] See below, pp. 75 *et seq.*

committee procedure. Sir Oliver Franks gives two prime examples: "The meeting might be fairly clear about what it thought should be done but gave insufficient attention to how it was going to be done and who should do it, or escaping this error, made another, and failed explicitly to allocate responsibility for instructing action among those present at the meeting. In either case the purpose of the meeting was frustrated; nothing happened."[1] Finally of course, each representative strives his utmost to secure decisions that will entail the minimum of change in his own department's policy. This is the truth behind Mr Balliol Scott's remark: "The ... interdepartmental committee, whether as a buffer between the conflicting sovereignties of several departments or as a coupling to prevent their independent and inconsistent action tends to achieve co-ordination only in terms of the lowest common denominator of agreement."[2]

Yet this is remarkably exaggerated, it quite overlooks the role of such Committees as the veritable forges of *policy*. If a Department has a policy, certainly it will try to stick to it. The great significance of the Interdepartmental Committee however arises when Departments have, not policies, but *views*.The Committees will be composed of representatives of departments, trained in committee work and anxious to arrive at some solution. In the end, though nobody quite knows how it was done, a *policy* is arrived at. This may then be considered by a top-level official Committee, or even a Ministerial Committee and the Cabinet itself. But much will never go this far: how far it goes is not even always determined by its intrinsic importance. The interests of Ministers or the clamour of the House are just as significant. Thus policy is being made all the time; and, subject to knowing generally how Ministers feel, and to direction on those specific matters to which the party in power is committed, it is the Interdepartmental Committees which make the great mass of it, and it is here that the influence of a Co-ordinating Department like the Treasury, is at its most powerful.

[1] Experience of a University Teacher in the Civil Service, pp. 11-12.
[2] Select Comm. Est. Sub. Comm. D. 1946-7, p. 93.

BOOK III

THE

CONDITIONS OF ADMINISTRATIVE ORGANIZATION:

SPACE

FOREWORD

SERVICES AND AREAS

SO far this essay has dealt with government services and the way
they are integrated by the Cabinet, the Treasury and the
Departments. Below this, administration begins to make immediate
contact with the citizen. For the most part the agents of the Ministries are stationed in offices throughout the country. These are nearly
always grouped under local H.Q. officers, into 9, 10 or 11 "Regions".
The "Regional" staffs are of the rank of Assistant-Secretary
downwards—whereas the problems treated so far mostly concerned
the rank of Assistant-Secretary and *upwards*. The regional level is
the lowest level in the administrative process. It is all detail. One
would expect therefore that the need for consultation and co-
operation between the regional staffs of different ministries would be
even more pressing than at the higher levels. This is so. It is the
paramount problem of regional organization.

This word 'region' introduces a new concept. The discussion has
so far dealt only with services, it must now deal with *space*. Administration can be organized by reference to either.

The M.N.I.[1] is to have 1,000 local offices grouped in 11 regions,
themselves controlled by an H.Q. at London. All offices in all regions
will treat their clientèle in much the same way. The N.A.B.[2] also is to
have 1,000 local offices in 11 regions. Again, a uniform *national* administration is secured. But in each of the 11 regions the N.A.B. and
M.N.I. officials must collaborate with one another. They must also
collaborate with the regional Hospital Board, with the Ministry of
Labour, and so forth. Cabinet, Treasury and Interdepartmental
discussions have already integrated their main policies for the nation
as a whole. The administration of these several different services
must also be integrated inside each regional *area*.

Now it is possible to organize these services upon a purely
regional basis. Suppose each of the 11 regions to contain its own

[1] The Ministry of National Insurance.
[2] The National Assistance Board.

government which administered *all* the services but only over its own restricted area. The region would have an integrated administration but the national administration of any *one* of the services would be disintegrated into 11 different regional practices. By the first method every service tends to be executed uniformly between area and area, but in isolation from its fellow services *inside* each of the areas. By the second, every service tends to be executed differently between area and area but in collaboration with its fellow services *inside* each of the areas.

The first system arises when each *Ministry* administers its service in the areas it finds convenient with its own personnel. This is a *Centralized* service.[1] The second arises when each *area* administers its range of services through a government it finds convenient with its own personnel. This is *decentralization*.

Centralization is illustrated by the relation of the 1,000 offices of the M.N.I. or N.A.B. to their H.Q. office in London. Decentralization is illustrated by the relation of the Dominions to the Ministry of Commonwealth Relations. A less extreme form of decentralization exists in the Federal State relationships of the U.S.A. A much more limited form exists in Britain in the restricted autonomy of our local government councils. In Britain centralization, and local autonomy, i.e. decentralization, exist side by side, i.e. administration based on the uniqueness of the *service*, and administration based on the uniqueness of the *area*. Ideal administration must combine the two. It must secure coherent administration of different services in each area with uniform treatment between areas.

This explains the plan of the following chapters. Chapter 1 explains what the regional offices of centralized services must do to create a coherent administration inside each area, where *national* uniformity for each service has already been guaranteed. This leads naturally into Chapter 2 which describes how local councils readily provide such a coherent administration inside their areas. Why then centralize? The reason emerges in Chapter 3 which describes the national structure of British local government and explains the so-called "boundary problem". Is centralization the only way to overcome this? Chapter 4 forms a sort of pendant to Chapter 1 and explains the means adopted to secure uniformity between area and area where the local council has already achieved an integrated administration inside its area, i.e. it describes the central-local relationship.

[1] Cf. definitions in Book II, Chapter 1.

CHAPTER 1

CENTRALIZATION AND ITS PROBLEMS

"For what Man in the natural State, or Course of Thinking, did ever conceive it in his power, to reduce the Notions of all Mankind, exactly to the same Length, and Breadth, and Height as his own?"

Swift: A Tale of a Tub.

UP to 1934, when the Unemployment Assistance Act was passed, relief of the able-bodied destitute was administered exclusively by the local councils. Since then that service has been piecemeal transferred to a central authority. The process was completed by the National Assistance Act of 1948. Trunk roads, hospital services, road-traffic licensing, the generation and distribution of gas and electricity, have also been transferred within the last twenty years. Centralization replaces local autonomy. Thereby the central authority falls heir to the problems successfully met by local government, i.e. by administration on the *area* principle. The foremost problem is that of co-ordinating different services within the given area. It is here that the conflict between the service (or functional) basis and the area basis of administration is most apparent and intractable. Two other problems besides demand solution. Because the local authority is elected by, and governs over a *small* area, a restricted area, it is effectively *accountable* and *informed*.[1] Now the central authority, if it takes over the services of the local authority must also try to be equally accountable[2] and equally informed. These two problems need some discussion before the main problem of this chapter is tackled: for they have a very important bearing on the respective merits of centralization and local autonomy.

I

A device used by the central authority to obtain local knowledge

[1] The next chapter elaborates these characteristics.
[2] See below, pp. 83-86.

is the *Advisory council.* It is not always used. Sometimes a Ministry feels that it is sufficient to plant a civil servant in the locality, give him some responsibility, and let him acquire a knowledge of local peculiarities as he goes along. In the social services, however, (e.g. assistance or hospital services), and in services of economic provision (gas and electricity) an advisory council has become common form. When the U.A.B. was set up to undertake the relief of all able-bodied unemployed between the ages of 16 and 65, its intention was to make the scales of such relief as far as possible uniform over the whole country. Up till then the relief had been handled by the Public Assistance Committees of the local councils, i.e. by elected bodies. These administered first the "transitional benefit" and, when this was exhausted, public relief proper. They had been entrusted with transitional benefit, which was a *national* fund (public relief being raised from *local* rates), simply because they could adjust such benefit in the light of their local knowledge of rents, employment possibilities, local costs of living, etc. But the extent of relief varied from one P.A.C. to another. This was one reason for setting up a strictly national administration to impose *uniform* rates of benefit. Yet such knowledge as the P.A.C.s possessed was vital to the new U.A.B. The Act accordingly made provision for local advisory bodies, nominated by the U.A.B. from panels drawn up by local authorities and associations of employers and employees. They were to advise the local offices of the Board on questions affecting rent, allowances in rural areas and give "such advice as they think proper regarding local administration of the regions in their application to any special conditions peculiar to the locality", and were to try to co-ordinate the Board's activities with those of the local authorities and voluntary services. Now the Board hurried to impose its standard rates of benefit before these committees were set up. A sudden change in circumstances took place in thousands of households, and an explosion of resentful violence brought the administration to a halt. A "Standstill Order" was hastily introduced while the Committees were set up. On their advice the over rigid rent formula of 1934 was modified to meet local conditions—(though only within limits which the Board laid down beforehand). In 1937 they were asked to devise ways and means of reducing the "standstill" scales gradually, so as not to cause sudden hardships. The committees made the Board's administration a success. By 1939 their work was well nigh complete. In Lord Rushcliffe's words "The Board have set out with the intention of combining the benefits of centralized administration through a government department with the local knowledge and personal touch that local people can bring to bear upon the service."

Similar considerations governed the constitution of advisory committees to assist the British Electricity Authority in the construction of local tariffs and the sale of electrical appliances. These committees will be composed largely of representatives of local authorities and Trades Unions.[1] The Regional Hospital Boards are peculiar in that they are not merely advisory but fully executive also: but their make-up was defended precisely because of its local character—"You can hardly have," said Mr Key to his critics, "a more local body than *that*."[2] What must be the final example is to be found in the Regional Boards of Industry. These interpret the Board of Trade and local industrialists to one another and work closely with the D.I. Panels. They comprise representatives of the local employees and employers, together with regional representatives of the interested Ministries; while their chairman is nominated by the Board of Trade.[3]

II

All these committees are nominated. Their composition is at the mercy of a Minister. Except for the Hospital Boards they are advisory only. The local council is elected and has executive authority. It is fully accountable to the electors. The Advisory Board is accountable only to the Ministers. On this account they have come in for rough handling. Mr Hudson complained that the consultative councils of the British Electricity Authority had "no effective executive power", were "merely 'stooges' of the Minister", Mr Macpherson called them, "mere creations of the minister, pallid phantoms without any power or responsibility whatsoever."[4]

Of course, the regional officer of the Ministry or Authority is not irresponsible. His Ministry may be criticized in Parliament and his own personal misdeeds become the subject of a whole debate. But he is not *locally* responsible to his local clientèle or consumers. It is

---

[1] See Hansard, 24 June, 1947, cols. 231-56, also Clause 7 of the Bill.

[2] Hansard, 1 May, 1946, column 208.

[3] A very full account is to be found in 2nd Report Select Committee of Estimates 1946-7 ("Development Areas") p. xi, and minutes of evidence *passim*.

[4] Hansard, 3 Feb., 1947, columns 1428 and 1458. Cf. Hansard, 30 April, 1946, for Mr Willink's and Mr Messer's attack on Hospital Boards.

far easier to bring a local government officer to account than the regional Civil Servant because the Town Hall is near and Parliament distant. The criticism of centralized services revolves around the indisputable fact that its day-to-day decisions are far less easily attacked than those of local authorities. On this the Recommittal Stage of the Electricity Bill[1] is a most illuminating commentary.[2]

III

Local knowledge, and some sort of accountability can be provided by these devices. Far more difficult is the problem of making the centralized services march together inside each area. And it is far more fascinating because the problem illustrates so clearly the rival claims of "function" and "area", as a basis of national administration. Here are a number of inter-related services. The general operation of each one is controlled from London. Indeed the general operation of *all* is controlled by deliberations at Cabinet, Treasury and interdepartmental level. How are the myriad details which arise in the actual field operation of each to be meshed together in each of the regions? This problem is not peculiar to Great Britain. The U.S.A. with over 100 different sets of government areas used by 47 different agencies has experimented (unsuccessfully) with a Federal Co-ordinating Agency.[3] In France the prefect is nominally the head of all civil servants in his Department, and the claims of hierarchy and area would seem to be reconciled. In practice his control is nominal, and the French dilemma is acute.

Three conditions seem to be required to solve the problem. First, the civil servant in the field must be allowed to settle a defined range of decisions on the spot: there is no point in his being there, if he must refer everything to Whitehall. Secondly, his area must be identical with that of his "opposite number" in other services. Finally there must be a machinery of consultation and co-ordination within these areas.

On the whole the Ministries' chief regional officers or Comptrollers are of the Assistant Secretary level, and this illustrates how far they can take decisions on their own responsibility. (The Ministry of Health's Housing Officers however are at the Principal

[1] Hansard, 24 June, 1947, especially cols. 231-87.

[2] *Ibid.*, see especially Lt.-Col. Elliot's speech at col. 272-3.

[3] President's Rept. on Admve. Management 1936, "Federal Field Agencies".

grade, and so are the Local Commissioners and Utilization Officers of the Ministry of Agriculture.) Among the chief ministries that devolve powers are the Ministry of Agriculture and Fisheries, the N.A.B., the Ministry of Food, the Ministry of Health (for housing only) the Home Office (for Civil Defence) the Ministries of Labour, National Insurance, Supply, Planning, the Board of Trade, the Ministries of Transport and of Works, the G.P.O., and the Service ministries. Generally speaking, each division of any Ministry is headed by an Under-Secretary, and its work split into "branches" each headed by an Assistant Secretary. The Regional Organization forms one such division with an Assistant Secretary in charge of each Region. The matters they may deal with are specifically defined, the discretion naturally varying somewhat between ministries. An example or two will suffice to illustrate the general situation. The Regional Controller of the Board of Trade carries a staff of about 100.[1] So much work was devolved on him that the staffs "have not had time to digest all they have at present."[2] He has a Location section which advises industrialists on the suitability of the region for a factory site, and helps choose and "clear" that site. "Another section deals with the usual run of building licence and priorities work, derequisitioning, and so on". "Section No. 3 deals with work .. devolved from ... H.Q. to the Regional Offices. ... A large number of functions have been devolved: the issue of manufacturing licences; labour ... from the point of view of a scrutiny of cases in which it is desirable to defer men from call-up on industrial grounds, and so on".[2] "Our policy," said the witness, "is so far as we can, to settle policy at H.Q. and devolve the executive work to the Regional Offices." The Ministry of Health's Principal Housing Officers are authorized "within certain broadly defined limits" to approve local authorities' proposals for sites, tenders, and their housing plans "without reference to Whitehall".[3] The Ministry of Works delegates to its Regional Directors clearly defined powers to issue building licences. For the so-called W.B.A. licence (highest priority for labour and materials) they may deal with work costing under £1,000 and for W.B.B. licences, they may approve work costing between £1,000 and £20,000.

There are also *interdepartmental committees* for considering these priorities and these may issue on their own responsibility W.B.A.

---

[1] 2nd Rept. Sel. Comm. Estimates Sub.-Comm. C. "Development Areas", 1947. Q. 780.

[2] *Ibid.*, Q. 778. [3] *Ibid.*, Q. 28.

licences up to £20,000 and W.B.B. licences for work costing over £20,000! Other interdepartmental committees have been set up for specific purposes in the regions and many of these have a specific range of authority delegated to them. The Regional Distribution of Industry Panels for instance can approve without further reference all projects involving premises less than 5,000 square feet (except in the London and Birmingham areas).[1]

The first condition, a delegation of authority to the regional officer, is thus satisfied; though one may question whether the width of delegation is even yet sufficient. The second condition, the standardization of regional boundaries, is being met at the moment. Prior to 1939 few ministries had "regionalized". The G.P.O. and Road Traffic Licensing Commissioners and the Road Engineering Division of the Ministry of Transport were the notable exceptions. The outbreak of war saw the creation of the Civil Defence Regions and all departments were pressed to "deconcentrate" their work into such regions. In 1946 the Treasury set up an interdepartmental committee called the Regional Organization Committee, which devised a set of 11 Standard Regions and called on each Ministry to show cause why it should deviate from their proposed boundaries. The departments which deviate widely include the National Savings Committee, the Highways Division of the Ministry of Transport and (even more so) its Road Traffic Commissioners, and the G.P.O. The remainder differ from each other chiefly in their treatment of the Greater London and S.E. area—an anomalous area anyhow; over the rest of the country the differences consist of very minor fringes of territory. Almost without exception the ministries all use the same towns for their Regional Offices. The process of standardization has gone so far that the Ministry of Health which had proposed 16 Hospital Regions reduced them to 11 which bear a close resemblance to the Standard regions, and even the Gas Supply Areas have tried to approach them: and all use the regional capitals. The 14 Electricity regions do not come quite so close. It is not surprising that they, the Highways and Road Traffic Areas of the Ministry of Transport, and the G.P.O. should diverge so widely, because they are highly technical services and less plastic than the others: also with the exception of the first, they are the *oldest* of the regions.

The final condition is that within these Regions, the different officers co-operate. The conditions are as difficult as can be, for with

[1] Sel. Comm. Estimates 1946-7, "Development Areas", p. 15.

only one or two exceptions the regional chiefs are all of the same civil service status,—there is no equivalent of the French Prefect, no higher civil servant with special status who might act as a court of appeal on the spot. Any disagreement at the region means referring the problem back to London for a decision and only one civil servant need disagree and this will occur. If regional matters are to be kept regional and yet co-ordinated, the situation demands frequent consultation and some agreement on majority voting procedure. The local officers recognize this very fully indeed and they have the same incentive to get things accomplished as any inter-departmental committee at H.Q.—and of course, labour under the same disadvantages. Two examples will illustrate their approach to co-ordinated activity.

The first is a Distribution of Industry Panel. It is interdepartmental, its representatives including the Controllers of the Ministries of Labour, Planning, Supply, the Admiralty, and Trade, with Trade in the Chair. Others are invited as their interests warrant. The panel's decisions stand except in the instances noted above:[1] and the decision itself is taken by majority vote.

The other example is drawn from Housing. Here five ministries *must* co-operate if a single house is to be built. The result is a mesh of five formal interdepartmental committees. The Regional Building Committee ensures that the local authorities do not begin more houses than there is labour and materials in the Region to complete. The Regional Building and Civil Engineering Committee is largely concerned with applying the Essential Work Order, and maintaining contact with the local building industry. The Schemes Co-ordinating Committee is an "expediting" committee to secure an even flow of labour and materials to sites before work is held up. Finally the Sites Committee 'clears' sites for the local authorities, i.e. it ensures that no other department has claims on them before they are sanctioned. Intermeshed with these is the D.I. Panel. One must also appreciate that each of the five ministries concerned is interlinked with other ministries in so far as other aspects of their work are concerned. For example, the Ministry of Labour will be also represented on the Regional Board of Industry, on the inter-departmental Building Licensing Committee, and the Iron and Steel Labour Supply Committees.[2]

The arrangements are in fact masterpieces of improvisation. They

[1] P. 80.
[2] Cmd. 7225 of 1947, p. 327, Report 1939-46 of Ministry of Labour.

show what the Civil Service can do, unnoticed, if put to it. They are certainly not ideal. So much is recognized by the Head of the Civil Service: "the regional organizations have … expanded, and I do not think they have quite settled down yet and we want a good deal more experience before we can really make sure of the right ultimate form of that organization." But the moves so far are all in the right direction, and the enquiry set afoot by the O.M. division of the Treasury may now be expected to standardize them.[1]

[1] Sel. Comm. Est. Sub.-Comm. D. (O. & M.) 1947. Qq. 1668-1670.

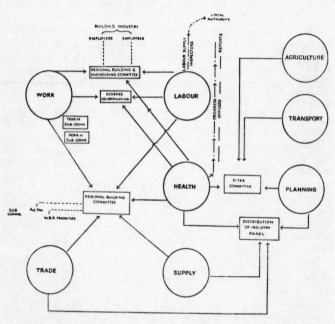

Regional inter-departmental Committees for Housing purposes.

CHAPTER 2

THE LOCAL COUNCIL

"Nature hath adapted the eyes of the Lilliputians to all objects proper to their view; they see with great exactness but at no great distance."

Swift: A Voyage to Lilliput.

AN alternative to the type of administration described in the last chapter is to entrust certain services to locally elected authorities each serving a certain area with its own officials. There are some 15,000 such councils and areas in England and Wales, staffed by over one million officials. If their trading services are ignored, their annual expenditure is about 700 million pounds, which is nearly one quarter that of the central departments.

Authorities may do only what the law expressly allows. Some of their functions are undertaken at their own pleasure: either by exercising some power permitted by general Act of Parliament (e.g. providing municipal restaurants, or entertainments) or else derived from express or specific Parliamentary sanction (either by the passing of a Private Act, or a Provisional Order, or by a minister's Special Order). Their chief and most expensive functions however are *obligations* created by general Statutes, and relate to Public Health, Planning, Police, Housing, Education and Roads.

The two primary patterns of such local administration are those of the County Borough and the County. The first is known as "one tier". A single council administers *all* the local services inside its area. In the "two tier" type, these functions are divided, between the County Council and the County District Councils. The County Borough's chief duties include Public Health, Planning, Police, Housing, Education and the care of its streets—*plus* any permissive powers it may have adopted or promoted in Parliament. The County Council has two distinct kinds of power. In the first place it directly administers the Personal Health Services, Education, Highways, Planning and Police. Secondly, it exerts an influence over the

"Districts". In consultation with the Districts it propounds schemes affecting the whole country, e.g. for the filling of M.O.H. vacancies, for the constitution of a Valuation Appeal panel. Next, it makes cash grants towards some District services, e.g. towards the salaries of full time M.O.H.'s, towards the provision of water and sewerage. Again, it acts as mediator in certain disputes between Districts, e.g. in their boundary disputes, or the recriminations of parishes against their Rural District Council. Finally, it may act in default of the District in respect of Housing and Public Health—their two most important duties.

These Districts may be non-county boroughs, or urban districts or rural districts. The chief distinction between the first two is of dignity; the borough possesses a Mayor and Corporation, the urban district a Chairman and Council. Their chief statutory duties are similar, viz. Public Health (environmental) and Housing. They differ from the Rural District chiefly in having more elaborate public health powers. The Rural District behaves very much in practice like a federation of parishes. These units have but rudimentary powers, no duties, and are valuable as being units of protest, and nuclei of organized opinion.

The Constitution of all these councils (excepting the rural parishes) is based upon the Municipal Corporations act of 1835. Since 1945, they have been elected by universal suffrage, almost (but not quite) identical with the Parliamentary suffrage. Both County and Non-county Boroughs are dignified by Mayors and Aldermen. The Council consists of directly elected councillors, with a 3 years' tenure, and Aldermen with a 6 years' tenure, who are elected by the councillors, in the proportion of one alderman to every three councillors. Each year one third of the councillors retire and new ones are elected while every 3 years one half of the Aldermen retire, and the body of councillors elect their successors. The County Council differs from this scheme in its less dignified titles (Chairman and Council) and by electing new councillors *en bloc* every 3 years. The Urban and Rural Districts councils comprise only elected councillors: there are no aldermen. One third of the Council is replaced every year. Finally, parishes under 300 strong have no council—all members meet together as a Parish meeting. Over 300 strong, they may elect a Council and even provide secret ballot. This is so expensive that election is usually by show of hands.

There are 83 County Boroughs, 61 Counties (exlcuding the L.C.C.) 309 Non-county Boroughs, 572 Urban Districts and 475 Rural

Districts; and about 14,000 parishes. The average population of a County Borough is 156,789, that of a County Council 406,726: of a Non-county Borough 29,650, of an Urban District, 14,163, of a Rural District, 15,856. This gives an appearance of logic which is totally false; but it does illustrate that, although all the councils are elected and constituted on a common pattern, their population varies very greatly. This makes description of their actual operation highly particular. The analysis which follows is therefore concerned with the big authorities—County Boroughs or County Councils.

II

The first great advantage which such local bodies possess over the regional H.Q.s of central ministries is their local knowledge. The local area and population is small enough for the officials as well as the councillors to know it intimately. Nevertheless difficulties do arise: some county boroughs have an enormous population. In the Metropolitan area the problem was tackled by adopting "two-tier" government, i.e. sharing the local services between the L.C.C. and 28 Metropolitan borough councils. In their 2nd Report,[1] the Boundary Commissioners suggested that the proposed Greater Liverpool and Greater Manchester, with populations of over 1 million apiece would be too large for single tier government and should be modelled on the L.C.C. pattern.

The difficulties are far more common in county administration where distance as well as population works against intimacy of administration and electorate. To-day it arises in a more acute form than before. Formerly the districts administered the majority of the county services, now the county council itself does so. This is "county centralization". It exactly parallels the centralization of Chapter 1, but on a Lilliputian scale. Various devices exist to overcome the remoteness of the County Council and its lack of knowledge. Education is actually *administered* by Divisional executives or "excepted districts" under the general control of the County Council. The first are appointed bodies consisting of the County Councillors for the areas concerned, plus representatives of the district councils of the districts falling inside those areas, and, finally, of others co-opted by the County Council. The second are the elected

[1] Rept. of Local Government Boundary Commission for 1947 (H. of C. 86), 1948.

councils of the districts nominated as "excepted". A similar device is to be found in the Guardians Committees set up to administer Poor Relief by the Act of 1929.[1]

Another device is that of delegation. Some County Councils delegate the care of roads to their Rural districts which act as their local agents. It is expected that the Planning powers of County Councils (under the 1947 Act) will be delegated likewise. In some counties certain powers, e.g. scavenging, are delegated to so called "parochial committees" which usually consist of the parish councillors together with the rural district councillors for those parishes and the county councillors for that part of the county.

Although comparable, these difficulties are clearly not so serious as those of a fully centralized service. The widest county is only a quarter the size of the average Region, and H.Q. at London must be apprized of all information in *all* the regions. Finally the councillor *must* be a resident of his district, and for the most part the bulk of local officers are home grown.

III

The Local Council's second great advantage is that it is an "omnibus" or many-purpose authority: the regional H.Q. is single purpose. The one can co-ordinate all its services and inform them with a single collective will: the other is a factious republic where all services are equals, and all common action is subject to veto, i.e. an appeal "to ministers". Yet to say the local council *can* co-ordinate is not to say councils habitually do so. The need for co-ordination in central government (see Chapter 1 above) was created by its Bigness. Bigness acts in the same way on local councils. The more people they administer the more complex their organization and hence the greater their tendency to disintegrate. They also must perfect means of co-ordination and for this they are not nearly so well equipped as the central administration.

Local Councils are *not* Houses of Commons, though some do have a very large membership—the L.C.C. has 166, the Lancs. C.C. 137, Liverpool 156, Manchester 144. They are amateur, unpaid, part time service. In the Counties and Rural Districts, distance from home creates a further obstacle to full time attendance so that in towns meetings are held usually once a month and in the Counties

[1] Now extinguished by the National Assistance Act of 1948.

once a quarter. The council is not a Parliament, because it meets intermittently and for short intervals. Secondly, although there are systems of party discipline, they are nowhere except in the L.C.C., comparable with the Commons.[1] This, and the intermittence of meetings has thwarted the development of a Cabinet system. Secret juntas do of course exist, sometimes on a party basis (these are usually Labour), sometimes on a "local influence" basis (mostly Conservative); but these are "grey eminences" (if eminence is the right term) and have neither constitutional status, nor formal responsibility. Only in London County with $3\frac{1}{2}$ million inhabitants does the Cabinet system exist and even there in an etiolated form. Thirdly, there is for the officials no effective equivalent of the Treasury, i.e. no administrative focus. Finally the work of the council is limited to specific services, whose principles have been settled by Parliament: the council is face to face with detail and execution. Hence the council as a whole only *supervises* the actual detail of administration. Execution is carried out not by itself but by its Committees, and it supervises by acting as a kind of Court of Appeal. The Council's relation to the Committee is that of a back-seat driver. One is almost tempted to say that the Council is to the Committee what back-benchers are to the Government.[2] The Committee is the workshop of local government. The relation of committee to committee constitutes the Council's problem of co-ordination.

Committees are of two kinds, permissive and statutory. Any council may set up a committee for any purpose, determine its size and constitution, and delegate to it any powers short of raising a rate or loan. This power is a most flexible and noteworthy instrument. It makes councils readily adaptable to new responsibilities and sudden circumstances: it is also unfortunately an easy way out for harassed or muddled councils where committee and sub and sub-sub- committees pyramid and proliferate. Some committees however *must* be set up. This represents the impact on local administration of central ministries anxious to superintend their broods. Thus county councils and county boroughs must set up Committees for Fire, Mental Deficiency, Allotments, M. and C. Welfare, Public Health, and Children. In most instances the council as a whole may act only upon their reports. Sometimes they must contain a certain proportion of co-opted persons of various types.

[1] Warren's *Municipal Administration*, Chapter 14.
[2] Cf. Finer, *Local Government*, p. 222.

Some committees are specially protected by their constitution, notably Watch Committees; the Councils cannot reject their financial estimates.

The committees meet far more often than the councils: to superintend the actual administration, to quiz, bait and badger their permanent officers, to sign cheques and receipts, and to formulate policy. They tend to parallel the permanent administrative departments of the council, though usually there are far more committees than departments. This means that the committees are usually served by the head of one particular department and they transact their business with him. Their relation may be a mutual harmony, the domination of one by the other, or simply, mutual exasperation. They vary in fact between the mathematical combinations possible to any dual relationship, not excluding courtship and marriage: and for the same reason. Furthermore by constantly working and meeting together in isolation from their fellows the committees develop a powerful sense of self-sufficiency and *esprit de corps*.

The whole system tends to an extreme disintegration. The committees are usually of varying sizes, and this gives the larger ones a heavy advantage over the smaller when it comes to voting on their proposals in full council. The distribution of functions does not always follow a logical pattern, custom and personal ambition playing a large part. A comparison of the committee structure of any number of councils shows remarkable dissimilarities outside the statutory committees. The existence of these introduces rigidities into the administration—they must exist, and so the other committees tend to be erected around them; they prevent the local authority from grouping its services as it thinks most desirable. Finally the councils—especially the County Councils which meet seldom—tend to delegate very wide powers indeed to their committees and in many cases retain no control over them—except a general financial one, coupled with a demand for annual—sometimes quarterly—reports. Some pretend that this practice is praiseworthy in that it leaves detail to committee and "principles" to the whole council. *E ben trovato, ma non e vero* for councils are often too large to debate general principles and in any case, individual councillors tend to pick on details for their public debate. The alternative is to re-examine in full council all that the committees do. This is impracticable for County Councils as they cannot meet often enough. In Boroughs the attempt has so congested the council's time that it has largely been abandoned.

The biggest councils have given much attention to the problem and many devices are used for securing coherent administration among the committees. Much can be achieved by carefully framed standing orders. Some provisions are general, e.g. they may nominate certain councillors as *ex officio* chairmen of certain committees; they may insist that committees seek the council's approval for any changes in policy. They may institute common procedures for the purchase of civic lands, and for the breaking open of highways. The "Instructions to Committees" contained in S.O.s have a similar effect, e.g. they may limit the sums that committees may spend without prior approval, or detail the matters where certain other and specified committees must be consulted. The effectiveness of S.O.s however is itself a function of the self discipline of councillors and the efficiency of the clerk's staff. These take the minutes at all committee meetings and are therefore competent to point out breaches of S.O.s. At the same time the centralization of all minutes of all committees in a single office enhances the position of the Town Clerk over all other heads of departments. His department is a focal point for all co-ordination: and this for two reasons. By controlling and keeping minutes the Clerk alone is in a position to know what all committees are up to, at all times. Secondly, what local authorities may or may not do is so hedged in by the law, that a wise council will hardly move a step without consulting their Clerk. An efficient Clerk's department will play in the local councils, the same co-ordinative role, the role of a "collective memory" that the Secretariat does to the Cabinet.

A second group of devices depends on the duties allocated to Committees just as among the central departments. Nearly all large councils have special functional committees, e.g. for Staff and for Finance, while their departments are similarly constituted. The Clerk's office will minute and print for the other departments, the Staff Department control establishments and the Treasurer the Estimates, and perhaps central purchasing also. Some councils centralize all property matters in one department, or all stores in their Works Department or central workshops in the Transport Department.

A third group depends on the membership of committees. It is possible to adopt a policy of cross-membership; indeed, to some extent of course, it is actually impossible to avoid, but some councils try to allot the members scientifically. Sometimes this device is reinforced by a joint sub-committee of two or more committees either reporting back to the parent committees or itself granted executive authority.

These devices are all at the inter-committee level. They would prevent two committees outbidding each other for a piece of land, or ensure that streets were not continuously broken open by different departments. Most large councils—e.g. Manchester with over 30 Committees and over 100 sub-committees—obviously feel the need for a central policy making organ also. The question does not arise for a R.D.C. with its four committees. The mammoth authority needs a small body not only to prevent committees overlapping, but to see that their policies are informed by a common purpose, to translate this into financial terms and to ensure that they are not formed solely with a view to temporary expediency but take due account of future needs. The L.C.C. has a "General Purposes Committee" to do this. "Every new proposal as to its bearing on the law of the land or on the Council's general line of policy or on its financial policy" must be discussed there. Some authorities have tried to use the Finance Commitee for this purpose. This can control the other committees in full council only by the personal prestige of its committee members, just as the Chancellor's supremacy depends on his personal pre-eminence in the Cabinet. Councillors have a sturdy sense of equality and some authorities carry this so far that all councillors are *ipso facto* members of the finance committee. In these authorities financial control becomes like the Caucus race in "*Alice*". Oxfordshire used for its Policy Committee a Selection or General Purposes Committee. Consisting of the chairman of all important committees it selected the committee men for all committees and also exercised a general surveillance over them. In addition their Finance Committee was made the more independent by excluding from it all Chairmen of Spending Committees.

Such selecting committees as these vary in shape and effectiveness from one authority to another. Here it suffices to note the need. Certainly the local authority is able to pursue a self consistent policy more easily than the regional H.Q.s—if only because of its smaller area and the interlock between committees and council. Yet it was necessary to show that even the local council has a problem of co-ordination, otherwise the superiority in this respect of the council to the regional H.Q.s—which I firmly believe to exist—would have been dangerously over-simplified. As soon as they grow large they must co-ordinate, just as *mutatis mutandis* the central administration must. This is not surprising. Exactly the same problem and much the same kind of solutions occur in "big business". All three reflect the increasing diseconomies of scale and the division of labour.

IV

There remains one final point of comparison between the regional organization and local government, viz. *accountability*. In local government this is obviously part of the relationship of electorate and councillor. Mistaken policy or flagrant maladministration can be corrected at the polls; aired in full council and publicized in the local press. The Nemesis of local maladministration is swift and direct. The Town or County Hall permits the groaning ratepayers or angry mothers to confront their tormentors directly. Desks can be thumped or threats bandied, because they are *voters*. They may thump the desk at Regional H.Q. also (when they have found it!)—but with how much less assurance! The Civil Servant is cushioned against their wrath by distance and time—distance from Westminster and the time it will take to make the explanations and counter-explanations that will culminate, only rarely, in an oral question on the floor of the House.

Yet one singularity is most notable. If a central Department is mismanaged, the Minister goes and the permanent head stays. If a local authority's Department is mismanaged, the Committee stays and the permanent head goes! This brings the argument back to its starting point—Councils are not Parliaments. First, they are part time and amateur and so the public credits the local officer, not the Committee, with day to day administration. Next, the officer is appointed at the council's pleasure and his tenure is not hedged about by any of the customary anonymity or permanency of the Civil Servant. Finally, the council itself actively administers, Parliament only controls and supervises active administration. In the central government, Civil Servants became anonymous and permanent when the Minister became responsible and dismissable: and he became such when the House broke into Government and Opposition parties. In local government the Civil Servant is personalized and impermanent because his Committee is neither collectively responsible to the council nor dismissable by them. It is neither, because it is bi-partisan, a microcism of the council itself. This is itself possible because although some councils consist of two parties many do not, and many more have parties which are largely nominal. Local Councils in no way reproduce the Cabinet-Commons relationship. They resemble the French Chamber under the 3rd Republic. They operate as though the Commons had no ministers but broke itself up into 30 Select Committees who collectively instructed and informed the permanent heads of the Departments.

THE BOUNDARY PROBLEM IN LOCAL GOVERNMENT

"Poor Nations are Hungry and Rich Nations are proud: and Pride and Hunger are ever at variance—"

Swift: Voyage to the Houynhnhms.

I

THE weakness of English local government is due neither to any inherent vice in local autonomy nor to the way individual authorities are constituted. It derives from the inter-relations of present day areas, functions and categories of council, and the impact on them of those social changes already described.

There are in England and Wales six categories of local authority. Their duties are defined in terms of their category. These categories however are *NOT* determined by the rational considerations of size, wealth and population. They are determined by an historic illogic, which stopped in 1888—the year when the single tier and double tier dyarchy of County Boroughs and County Councils was created. So, in the first place, each category overlaps its neighbours, and there are County Boroughs whose populations and wealth are equalled or surpassed by non-county boroughs and urban districts. In the second place each category contains within itself the most striking divergencies of wealth and population, as the table on page 94 shows. Now *wealth* depends on the assessed net annual rental of occupied real property in each area: it is completely local and being based on real property, cannot migrate. Hence a third element of weakness, in that any alteration of boundaries between local authorities also alters their resources. This is the root of the sterile wrangling between county and county borough from the Onslow Commission of 1923 to the Boundary Commission of 1947. Money has been the root of all evil but "tediousness the limbs and outward flourishes".

So *Functions* consequently bear little or no relation to *area* and *wealth*, i.e. to capacity to administer: while boundary adjustment to equate areas and riches has been piecemeal, slow, and increasingly resisted by the counties. On this ramshackle structure bursts the full flood of social and economic change. Space shrinks and populations move. By 1919 it was clear that:

		Area in acres	Population	Product of 1d. rate
County-	Largest:	51147	1063000	29125
Boroughs	Smallest:	4690	23780	855
Non-county	Largest:	8783	178590	7600
Boroughs	Smallest:	3390	876	12
Urban	Largest:	12559	211550	8550
Districts	Smallest:	1648	707	16
Rural	Largest:	34653	79940	1102
Districts	Smallest:	11855	1200	98
Counties	Largest:	148691	2186000	88143
	Smallest:	97273	17820	466 [1]

(a) Many areas were too small, too sparsely populated, and too *poor* to carry on the duties which their category imposed on them at the standard which Parliament had laid down.

(b) For technical reasons, some services demanded an area larger than the very largest that existed.

The structure has responded slowly to the first problem. The primary reason for the centralization of some services which hitherto have been locally administered lies in the failure to solve the second problem.

II

"We are of opinion that many of these authorities owing to their small population and the meagre amount produced by a penny rate are quite incapable of carrying out their public health duties properly. ... Even a moderate scheme of capital expenditure for the

[1] 1st Rept. Bdy. Commission, pp. 6-7.

building of houses, for a new water undertaking, or a new sewerage scheme seems enormous to them, and the interest on a loan, viewed in the light of the product of a 1d. rate, looms tremendously large. ... Moreover these small Authorities of necessity cannot obtain the services of the best type of official. ... We are of opinion that the variations in the standard of services rendered with regard to housing water, sanitation, supervision of milk and meat, disinfection, scavenging, etc., are due to the fact that the districts vary so considerably in size, population and financial resources... ."[1] Thus reported a Committee of Enquiry into the Anti-Tuberculosis Service in Wales. Over the whole report broods the stench of the sickbed, squalor, dirt, dung heaps and lingering death. The problem of areas is an exercise in human miseries. There are still too many of these dwarf authorities. Among 309 non-county boroughs, 127 have a penny-rate product less than £400; among the 572 Urban Districts there are 424, among the 475 Rural Districts, 338. These authorities are still entrusted with the environmental public health services—not only the most expensive of all the services of social provision but the most vital. Fifteen years ago their functions were much more extensive than to-day and often included primary education,[2] the child health services,[3] town and country planning, the fire services, and sometimes, police.

How can this kind of weakness be overcome? The least revolutionary method would be to confirm authorities in their present powers but make up their resources by discriminatory grants in aid from the central ministries. Next, such financial assistance could go together with a transfer of services from the smaller to the larger areas. Finally these methods could be combined with a programme of boundary adjustments. In point of fact, since, 1919, all three methods have been used simultaneously, but piecemeal.

Conditional grants of money from the National Exchequer developed slowly throughout the nineteenth century. In 1890 they were in the neighbourhood of some £6.5 millions only but in 1948-9 they totalled £407 millions! (A sum even larger than the total collected directly by the local authorities from rates, which is £308 millions). Clearly the grants alone make the present work of the

---

[1] Anti-Tuberculosis Service in Wales and Monmouthshire Enquiry, 1939; 388, 397, 404.

[2] Never the R.D.s: U.D.s over 20,000 and Boroughs over 10,000 in 1902.

[3] Attracted to the school service.

local authorities possible. Yet grants unaccompanied by any change in local government structure do not solve the problem. In the first place they would undoubtedly form so large a proportion of the poorer authorities' expenditure as to make those authorities independent in name only: for it must be remembered that the authorities' financial independence is their sole sanction for political independence. In the second place it calls for discriminatory grants, the sums being proportional to local needs. At present the Police and Road grants are percentage grants: the Ministry matches the local expenditure. Thus the richer the authority, the more it obtains from the Ministry. The Housing subsidy is a fixed sum per house, and so does *not* vary with need. (Although provision is made for areas with an exceptional rate burden.) The new Education grant is the difference between a fixed sum per pupil subtracted from the product of a 2s. 6d. rate—so that there is some relation to ability to pay. The only grant which is perfectly geared to local need is the new block Equalization grant. The rateable value of each authority is first ascertained; then it is "weighted" by reference to the sparsity of its population and the number of its school children. Next an average weighted rateable value for the whole county is obtained. The difference between its own and the national average weighted rateable value is credited to the local authority by the Ministry of Health. The sum it receives is this credited rateable value (times) its rate in the £. So the sum it receives is a product of its own poverty and its propensity to spend. This sum is recalculated every year and so extremely flexible. If the system were extended to *all* grants in aid there would be a certain guarantee tha authorities attracted grant in proportion to their poverty. But out of the £407 millions of national exchequer grants the Equalization grants account for £33 million only.

Consequently, the growth of grants has been accompanied by a steady shift of services from the county districts to the counties. Third-class roads were transferred in 1929: Education in 1944: Police and the Personal (including School) Health Services in 1946: Town and Country Planning and the Fire Services in 1947. The Districts are left with only the Governmental Health Services and Housing. The latter is very strictly controlled by the central government, and both are subject to the default powers of the county. The process of transfer has reached its limit unless the Districts are to be left with no powers beyond choosing flowers for their parks and sites for their cemeteries.

Even so, the problem has not been solved, nor will it be until each category of local authority is based uniquely on the criteria of finance, area, and population. What is the point of transferring Education from Urban Districts to County Councils when the *largest* Urban District has over 200,000 population[1] and raises £8550 by a 1d. rate, and the smallest County has only 17,820 people and can only raise £466 by a 1d. rate! The transfer from "less capable" to "more capable" authority is nominal only. It is impossible to re-allocate functions without also redrawing boundaries and impossible to redraw boundaries without affecting the wealth and population. The significance of the 2nd Report of the Boundary Commission was precisely this—that within two years from the day it was told to adjust boundaries, it realized that its task was not possible because: "We have no jurisdiction over functions".

Up to 1947 there had been certainly some boundary adjustments. From 1888 to 1923, as population drained from countryside to the towns the number of county boroughs (i.e. boroughs with over 50,000 inhabitants), increased continually. Thereby the county areas were eroded, and lost wealth and population to authorities which were independent and paid no county precept. By the creation or enlargement of county boroughs the counties between 1888-1923 lost 15.74 per cent of their population and 13.82 per cent of rateable value. Their protests before the Onslow Commission (1923-9) checked the tendency. The population necessary to warrant the creation of a county borough was raised first to 75,000 then to 100,000. The war postponed a review of the county borough's proposals, and to meet them quickly a Boundary Commission with executive authority was set up in 1945 to peregrinate, to examine, and to make Orders. The ambition of the Boroughs, bottled up since 1923, now produced a ludicrous situation. In England alone their proposals (1945), fully adopted, would have reduced the counties' populations by another 26 per cent and their rateable value by $25\frac{1}{2}$ per cent. In the meanwhile, the 1929 Local Government Act had prepared for a reshuffling of District Boundaries—the so called "county review" which was to take place every 10 years. Many tiny urban districts were reabsorbed into the surrounding Rural District, and some larger ones were incorporated in boroughs, but the root of the problem was not touched.

The 2nd Report of the Boundary Commission (1948) was at once a commentary on the wretched progress of the past, and a starting

[1] 1st Report of the Boundary Commission, p.7.

point for any new proposals. It wished to create uniform categories of local authorities by reference to their population. (Its great weakness was precisely that it could not consider local finance.) To this end, England would be divided into two-tier authorities of between 200,000 and 1 million, and one-tier authorities of 200,000 to 500,000. These would consist (i) of the existing counties suitably sub-divided or united, and (ii) of those county boroughs with over 200,000 population. Both kinds of units would be called" Counties".

In the two-tier counties, the county districts would continue to exist, after their boundaries had been reviewed, with much the same functions as at present. In between them and the County Council, a *new* type of intermediate authority would be created, viz. of towns with 60,000 to 200,000 inhabitants. These would be autonomous in respect to education and health; for other services however they would form part of the county. This new intermediate authority is cunningly and confusingly called a "county borough". This category would be recruited from the present county boroughs of less than 200,000 population, and the present non-county boroughs and urban districts of more than 60,000.

Whatever the demerits of this particular scheme it would create a logical set of categories in local government, and allow what is not now possible, the correct matching of populations and functions. In conjunction with discriminatory grants-in-aid and the transfer of functions, the difficulties of local administration within the *existing areas* (i.e. the "new" counties) would be largely overcome. Now these are difficulties soluble within areas of 1 million population (the Commission's figure), i.e. a population of about *double* the existing county. It offers no solution for the problems of the second category (see below), i.e. those which demand an area larger than the largest of the Commission's proposed areas.

III

Some services need an area larger than the County for purely technical reasons. Trunk roads should not vary in width and surface and lighting as they pass from one county frontier to the other. The supply of water depends on geological catchment areas. The conservation of rivers and their freedom from pollution calls for a single authority over their whole course. The licensing of road traffic depends on economic concentrations. Hospitals demand an area larger than the County because the shrinkage of administrative space has transformed them from being local and self-regarding matters into national ones—a process first recognized by the R.C. on Local Taxation of 1901, and repeated by the Interdepartmental Committee in 1914.[1] Education, public health, police and fire prevention no longer concern each local area alone. There is an insistent pressing demand for a national minimum, a national flat rate. This view tends towards ever larger areas and logically stops short only at our coasts.

Hence there is a clamant demand for ever wider areas of administration, ever wider areas of charge. If local government is to be retained, then either the counties and county boroughs must voluntarily combine their services, or new and larger local government areas must be created. The alternative is the complete supersession of local administration and the centralization of the Service. Now the failure of the local government structure to respond in either of the first two senses is the main, if not the sole reason for the centralization noted in Chapter 1.

Nearly every Statute which imposes duties on local authorities makes provision for the joint operation of the service by any number of them. The response has been pitiful. Local patriotism without which local government is impossible has by very excess made local government inefficient. In addition the financial basis of joint undertakings raises acutely the question, "Why should '*we*' pay for '*them*'?" The mechanics of such disputes emerged clearly in 1939 when the Welsh authorities sought to alter the basis on which they contributed to the Edward VII Trust, the association which provided the anti-tuberculosis service for the whole of Wales. The existing basis was half by ability to pay (roughly represented by their rateable value), and one half by user (roughly represented by population). This satisfied nobody. Some authorities demanded that each should pay the exact cost of the services rendered, others that each should pay in proportion to the extent of T.B. in their area, a third group demanded that rateable value be the criterion, a fourth that there should be a uniform rate. Each one suggested the basis which gave it most and cost it least.[2] The Edward VII fund was by then too well established to be destroyed, and the dispute was settled by central intervention; but it can be understood that such considerations have

[1] Cd. 638, of 1901; Cmd. 7315 of 1914.

[2] Enquiry into Anti-Tuberculosis Service in Wales and Monmouthshire, pp. 191-193.

prevented countless schemes from ever operating and caused many others to collapse.[1]

Failing amalgamation by agreement, the creation of new super counties has been urged, under the various names of Provinces or Regions. It is impossible here to analyze the very many projects put forward.[2] Professor Cole has suggested the grouping of refurbished counties and county boroughs, into Regions each averaging some 1 to 2 million people, and these into 10 Provinces whose directly elected Councils would have planning and co-ordinating duties, but not executive ones. A somewhat similar proposal was put forward by the N.A.L.G.O. except that their "Regions" were to range from 100,000 to 500,000; their "Provincial" Council is to be indirectly elected. The various local government authority associations have each put proposals forward. The County Councils want to extend two-tier government by incorporating all the county boroughs under 200,000 population; i.e. they want to perpetuate their own existence. The county boroughs want to extend except where "inappropriate". They were prepared to leave such areas to "two-tier" administration, i.e. to the plundered and defeated County Councils. Urban districts strongly objected to large extensions of county boroughs (i.e. they declined to be swallowed up) and the non-county boroughs also favoured two-tier government provided enough services were entrusted to the "county districts"; they suggested that the Boundary Commission should allocate these, not the County Councils. The Rural districts spoke in the same vein—they supported two-tier government provided they were enlarged at the expense of smaller boroughs and urban districts, and allowed to administer services in their own right and not by mere delegation. They strongly opposed the encroachments of expanding County Boroughs.[3] It would be hard to find a more revealing picture of interest-begotten prejudice masquerading as the public weal.

In a sense the 2nd Report of the Boundary Commissioners marked a move *away* from Local Government Regionalism as put forward by N.A.L.G.O. and Professor Cole. It proposed that the new counties (which term includes some former county boroughs)

[1] Scott Report, Cmd. 6378/1942, para. 148; *A National Water Policy.* Cmd. 6515 of 1944, p. 25; and especially Appendix C to *A National Health Service* notably at p. 78. Cf. also *Joint Authorities* in C. H. Wilson, "Essays on Local Government" (B. Blackwell) 1948.

[2] *Appendix A* to "Essays on Local Government."

[3] 2nd Report Bdy. Commission, pp. 151-6.

should have populations of between 200,000 to 1 million people. Since many existing county boroughs will sink back into the counties under the title of *new*-county-boroughs, this new pattern is easily arrived at by:

(*a*) Leaving 20 County Boroughs with their present status;

(*b*) *Amalgamating* two or more existing counties into 6 new two-tier counties;

(*c*) *Dividing* 4 existing two-tier counties to make 11 new ones.

In short the Report turned its back upon any suggestions of super-counties, provinces or regions. It had to work by minor adjustments to the existing frontiers. It proposed a scheme by which local government categories would bear a logical relation to area, wealth and population, and that is all. The problem of the supra-county services remains quite unsolved. But it is *pressing*. Voluntary amalgamation has failed. Creation of larger democratically elected authorities is hotly disputed, and officially discountenanced. Into the gap flows the Ministry. It takes out of the hands of the local authorities their control of traffic licensing (1930), trunk roads (1936 and 1946), public assistance (1934 and 1948), hospitals (1946), electricity distribution (1947), gas generation and distribution (1948), valuation of rateable property (1948). It administers them itself inside 10 to 14 huge regions. Thereby the services which technically demand larger areas find their needs met—by centralization.

There still remain some services like Education, Town and Country Planning, Public Health, Police, Housing, which have a national bearing and yet are administered by locally-elected bodies. They are quasi-national services. Why are they not also administered direct from Whitehall? The answer is that the authorities *themselves* are subject more and more to direction as well as to control. The administration of these services illustrates *another* kind of centralization, a sort of local-central *partnership*.

CHAPTER 4

THE CENTRAL-LOCAL RELATIONSHIP

"... *If any Town should engage in Rebellion or Mutiny, Fall into violent factions, or refuse to pay the usual tribute; the King hath two methods of reducing them to obedience* ..."

Swift: A Voyage to Laputa.

THESE "quasi" national services can on the whole be ad-ministered quite efficiently by the average county or county borough: but the national interest, and fair play, demands a standard of administration uniform over the whole country. The Ministries sponsoring the service tacitly admit that as an engine of administration the local council is superior to a Regional H.Q. The existence of sub-average areas is countered by giving ministries power to amalgamate such units into larger ones (*cf.* the Police, Fire Service, and Town and Country Planning Acts, 1947). The problem which remains is: to secure uniformity of standard between one area and another. Chapter I described a system which guaran-teed uniformity between areas, but at the possible expense of incoherence inside each area. The present system provides coherence inside each area: it remains to secure coherence between each area. This represents a *degree* of centralization whereas the former system represents centralization pure and simple.

The nineteenth century saw real local autonomy, i.e. extreme decentralization, in the so-called local services. It was most marked for public health and roads, less so for police and education, and very much less so in regard to public assistance. The Parliament of 1835 which passed the Municipal Corporations Act was obsessed not by the sluggardliness of local authorities but by fear that they would go too fast and too far. To this, the Alderman principle found in the County and Borough Councils bears silent witness to-day. The keynote of Goschen's "assigned revenues" of 1888 (by which certain national revenues were earmarked in perpetuity for local authorities) was a desire to be quit of the local councils, to let them go their own way independent of the central government.

Within ten years the revolution in communications was in full swing. By 1946 the whole concept of local self-regarding functions, as one finds it in J. S. Mill[1] was obsolete. The 1901 Royal Commission on Local Taxation was forced to recognize that some services carried out by the local authorities, viz. Poor Relief, Education, Police and Main Roads were "national" not local. The interdepartmental Committee of 1914 commented: "this process of 'nationalization' is still going on ... main roads and education are more national in character than at the date of that[2] Report ... ." By 1946 the personal health duties of local authorities were described as part of the *National* Health Service; the first clause of the Education Act of 1944 gave the Minister the duty to "secure the effective execution by local authorities under his control and direction of the *national policy*." The first clause of the Water Act (1945) made the Minister "secure the effective execution by water undertakings under his control and direction of a *national policy* relating to water." Parallel with this shift of emphasis went the explosion of the 1835 myth. With the exception of one or two dynamic authorities, the local administration was far behind the demands of Parliament. Sluggish and inert it was most often "parsimony tempered by patronage". By the end of the Second World War the local authorities were considered less as councils in their own right than as mere local instruments of departmental policy.

The relationships between central and local authority have therefore undergone a transformation. To a large extent they are still nineteenth century instruments and are only now being refurbished to play their new part. They were devised to persuade and control local authorities whose duties affected chiefly themselves, and which Parliament suspected might be dangerously radical and waste the rate payers' money. Most central local links to-day are therefore either persuasive or deterrent. Among the "persuasive" powers there is first of all the publication of reports and circulars, and the provision of expert assistance. Sometimes the Ministry act also as a Court of Appeal in certain cases, e.g. in disputes between one Local Education Authority and another. The early nineteenth century Radicals, trusting in "reason", considered that the mere force of good examples would promote efficiency in municipal administration

The "deterrent" powers are far more significant. One important

---

[1] Representative Government, Chapter XV.
[2] I.e. the 1901 Royal Commission Report already cited.

example is the control of local authorities' loans. These may be raised only under the authority of some Statute, and in each case the Ministry of Health and other interested departments must approve. Loans are vital for any capital expenditure, i.e. for any building construction or municipal trading services. The control of borrowing, designed originally to prevent the waste of public money, is very frequently used by the Ministry of Health to lay down standards of probity and sobriety in local authorities' accounting. It becomes a retrospective check on irregularities.

A second power is the right of ministries to insist on specific qualifications for certain kinds of local officials. Appointments as the Chief Education Officer or the County Chief of Police must be approved by the Ministry of Education and Home Office. Qualifications are laid down for M.O.H.s, Sanitary Inspectors, Inspectors of Weights and Measures, and Certified Teachers.

Thirdly, the ministries possess important sanctioning powers. For example the Ministry of Town and Country Planning must approve "Development plans" under the Act of 1947, the Home Office must approve Fire Service Schemes, and many ministries have the right to make compulsory purchase orders, if they are satisfied that the authorities claims are good. Bye-laws must always receive a ministerial sanction before becoming operative, those for "good rule and government" by the Home Office, others by the interested department.

Finally, there is *audit*. The Ministry of Health has a staff of 83 District Auditors. The boroughs are privileged in that they need only present their Housing, Public Assistance, Education and National Health Service accounts to the District Auditors. All other authorities must present *all* accounts. The audit is minute and exhaustive. It exists to detect illegal or unaccountable expenditure and, since the Poplar Case,[1] expenditure "so unreasonable as to be illegal". It is a most penetrating review of maladministration for its sanction gives pause to the boldest councillor: this is a *personal* surcharge to the extent of the inadmissible expenditure. It is true that the Ministry of Health or the High Court may remit or quash the surcharge if under £500, and the High Court if *over* £500: but then again, they may *not*, and any Councillor may find himself personally liable. Consequently, councillors increasingly tend to consult the Auditor before embarking on any expenditure which is novel.

[1] Cf. Finer, *English Local Government*, 2nd edition, pp. 322 *et seq.*

These powers are sufficient to keep the boldest Council in check. But suppose they are not bold? Suppose they refuse to spend on the services which Parliament has obliged them to develop? The auditor cannot surcharge where an authority has not spent money; moreover the loan sanction presupposes that the authority wants a loan. The "deterrent" powers could stop a workhouse being badly conducted but they could not make two workhouses grow where none grew before. The nineteenth century had seen the problem as a central check on local prodigality, and in the twentieth century the public conscience expressed in Westminster was far far ahead of the local authorities'. Parliament wanted to goad not to restrain. For this some new type of sanction was necessary—a power that would make local authorities act. The local authority naturally had a *legal* obligation to carry out the law: but its sanction was either the clumsy writ *"mandamus"*, which was never in fact used, or the Ministry's cumbrous right to act in default and charge the authority with the cost. Something more flexible was needed.

Up to the Second World War this was provided by adapting the grant-in-aid to form an agency of *control*. For the grant-in-aid could be made conditional on a certain standard of administration. Some of the very earliest grants had this character, e.g. those for Education and Police. Both were accompanied by *Inspection*. Since Goschen's anachronistic attempt (in 1888) to make grants unconditional, every increase in grant and every new grant has been accompanied by conditions and inspection. This is clearly seen in the new Fire Service Act where the Home Office lays down a singularly detailed code of regulations, and backs them with inspection, in return for a 25 per cent grant. To-day, with grants running at £408 millions and exceeding the rate-raised totals, the Inspector can back his suggestions with the threat to withdraw the grant. No local council could afford that loss. Compliance is assured.

Thus Police, Fire Service, Education, Roads, Housing, Planning and Public Health administration all give conditional grants and ensure compliance with their *national* policy through a corps of inspectors. The administration remains local, but set in a general and national framework of control.

Such at least is the *theory*. In practice, despite the Inspectorates and grants-in-aid, administration tends to be very much more local than it is national. The Inspectorate cannot give the services a character that is national *enough*. Each department has its own inspectors and they co-operate little. Each has a different conception of the degree of control needed and this is reflected in the number of their inspectors. In 1939 there were only 2 police inspectors, 9 divisional Road Engineers, and some 80 odd public health inspectors. The last two corps were considered in the light of specialist advisors rather than "controllers". The most effective corps was the H.M.I. of Schools—numbering 340.[1] Yet even these were regarded as advisors rather than inspectors. Furthermore the efficiency of inspection is very limited. Even the H.M.I.s (the most numerous) could inspect primary schools only once in 3 years and Secondary Schools once in 7. Corps less numerous can inspect even less often. Indeed, the infrequency of inspection was a contributory cause of the O'Neil scandal which culminated in the Curtiss Report. Finally, the threat to withdraw the grant in aid is itself so cumbersome as rarely if ever to be used. The block grant for health services was never once withdrawn between its inception in 1929 and its demise in 1948. On the contrary. Four Welsh counties with disgustingly poor health standards openly used the grant, not to improve their services but to reduce the general rates.[2] The Curtiss Committee stated that often no action was taken on Inspectors' reports going back over a period of many years—either because he was not backed by his ministry or else because the local authority declined to act.[3] When in 1947 the Home Secretary threatened to withdraw Salford's police grant if its Council appointed a certain officer as their chief of police, the national press exploded with indignation, and the Home Secretary had not only to interview the officer personally but had to defend himself in a debate on the Adjournment. He won his point—but it was clearly shown how difficult it is to withdraw a grant.

Hence a new device designed to rivet upon the local authorities a far more effective control. This is the "development plan". Its origin lies in the schemes—as under the 1921 Education Act, or 1929 Local Government Act—which local authorities had to prepare for the central ministries' approval, before administering the service. Those required since 1944 are far more detailed than ever before. The best examples are to be seen in the Education Act of 1944 and the Town and Country Planning Act of 1947. In the Education Development Plan[4] the authority must specify into what category it proposes to

[1] "His Majesty's Inspectors." There are now 502. (Cmd. 7426, p. 8.)
[2] Anti-Tuberculosis Service in Wales, Enquiry, p. 411.
[3] *Op. cit.* p. 132.
[4] Education Act 1944, 7 and 8. Geo. VI, Clause 11 (2).

place each school within its area, the type of education to be given and the age-range of the pupils: the proposed alterations of any school and an estimate of costs: what additional schools will be required and where; what provision will be made for defectives or children under 5; what provision will be made for boarding schools and any ancillary matters such as school transport, meals etc. A completed plan runs to a whole volume. This scheme is submitted to the Ministry. Amendment takes place by negotiation. But once approved the Ministry makes a Local Education Order. From that moment, the scheme becomes binding law upon the authority.

The development plan procedure is an enormous jump forward in central control, and is most significant for the future. It would seem to weld together the advantages of local administration and central planning. The scheme emanates from local knowledge: the central ministry has to review it to see that it is up to national standards, and does not clash with the plans of its neighbours. The reviewed and amended plan is then handed back to local administration, i.e. the detailed execution is in the hands of a locally accountable body, an all-purpose authority which is also administering the housing, transport and health services with which educational policy must march. The Inspector's task is a simpler and more congenial one of getting the local authority to adhere to its own plan.

Of course the larger local authorities fiercely resent any such increased control. They feel they can work better without interference. Yet a complete local autonomy in Education, Police, Fire Prevention would be undesirable if not downright ridiculous, for these services are considerably more national than local. The local authority points with pride to its initiative: the Ministry might well point out that the trend of the nineteenth century had to be from "permissive" acts to compulsory duties. The local authority presses its local knowledge: the Ministry argues that it is often *too* local, it is "parochial". The authority point out its "all-purpose" character; the Ministry replies that this is ideal inside the area, but does not secure uniformity with sister areas. It goes on to show that completely autonomous provision is patchy, often non existent, of varying standard, and in many cases administratively wasteful.

Some national co-ordination there must be. There are only three alternatives, viz. voluntary co-operation by local authorities, which is impracticable, complete supersession of local authorities which is undesirable, or a central local partnership. Hitherto this partnership has tended to confirm the local authorities in their autonomy. The development plan and stricter central control reflects the plain, if unfortunate fact that Britain is now "one vast neighbourhood unit", and the local authorities *agencies* of national administration.

What then are the criteria which ought to decide the degree of central control to which a service should be subjected? There seem to be three. If none are present, the service should be exclusively local; where all are present, exclusively central; where only some are present, there should be some form of local-central partnership.

The *first* condition is: that the service is of national and not local importance. This may mean either that local neglect adversely affects the whole nation, e.g. neglect of trunk roads; or it may mean that in the opinion of the local authorities the need for the service has been created by national policies and not local ones, and therefore the "nation" should assume their burden—e.g. A.R.P. duties. But in neither case does this first condition *alone* determine that a service must be administered by the central government, for either or both considerations might with equal justice be urged against the continued local administration of education, sewerage, or police. A second criterion must co-exist.

This *second* criterion is: that all citizens should enjoy similar standards. Yet even where this criterion is super-added to the first there still remain services such as education, police, and fire service which continue in local hands. A third condition is necessary to justify the outright supersession of local administration.

This *third* condition is: that the service cannot be greatly improved without aggregating the present units of administration. Such aggregation may be either geographical or functional. In the first, the technically best area for specialization and economy oversteps the existing local frontiers—as in hospital catchment areas. In the second, the technically best unit demands an amalgamation of public and private enterprises, e.g. as between voluntary and municipal hospitals, private and public gas or electricity undertakings. The Water Act of 1945 which tried to force private and public enterprises into compact local units by central government pressure, but which stopped short at "nationalizing" them, was an attempt to escape the conclusions implicit in the present analysis; and in so far as the Act hopelessly failed, and two political parties are pledged to outright nationalization of water supply and distribution, it may be taken to confirm the force of our argument.

BOOK IV

PERSONNEL AND THE PUBLIC SERVICE

———————

THE last two books dealt with "Structure". Yet "structure" is, simply, the *way* Civil Servants are employed, Just as the picturesque deployment of troops at Malplaquet gave way to the battle drill of Arnhem so the method of grouping and deploying civil servants has had to respond to new problems. Does our age need a new kind of Civil Servant as it does a new kind of soldier? So far this book has described how under the impact of scale, and the novel objectives of State activity, the administrators have been entrusted with greater responsibility, have had to specialize much more and consequently co-ordinate their work much more. What of the administrator himself? To what extent do his new tasks call for fresh skills, qualities and incentives?

The first two chapters which follow limit themselves to the Home Civil Service. The problems of the Foreign Service and the semi-public corporation have had to be left out. Even then discussion must centre around the administrative, i.e. policy making grade of the Home Civil Service. Space is too limited to discuss all grades and the Administrative Class is the most significant. Then the third chapter turns to the Local Government Service, which employs far more officers than the central Ministries, and has also felt the impact of the new conditions.

CHAPTER 1

THE BASIC FEATURES OF THE CIVIL SERVICE

"The Number of people increased."

Swift: A Voyage to Laputa.

I

IT has been fashionable to contrast the rigid formalized hierarchy of the Civil Service with the daring, the rapid promotions, the economic efficiency of Private Enterprise. If, as hitherto, Private Enterprise means a complex of highly competitive small firms producing for private profit, the Civil Service naturally appears *Monstrum horrendum, informe, ingens*, but I fail to find any validity in the comparison. The Civil Service is unique not because it is huge, but because it is a huge *unit*. Its million employees[1] are directed by a single management and paid by a single agency. To be valid, any comparison must be made not with the textile industry, for instance, and its 750,000 employees under dozens of competing managements but with say General Motors Inc. and its 250,000 employees under *one* management: not with a number of tiny competing establishments but with a commensurably large private enterprise *unit*. This has of course highly unpolitic consequences, for on the whole the most criticized aspects of Civil Service personnel policy are also the unsolved problems of Big Business. ...

Comparison is possible at three points, organization, personnel, and objective. In both enterprises, the size of the unit imposes those principles of structure which have so far formed the chief topic of this book and it is no accident that the Americans perfect "Theories of Organization" which draw from the common experiences of both. In so far as such organization is based on common principles, it possesses[2] similar problems of personnel management; but though the problems may be the same they are not always treated in the same way, since the two types of enterprise have an essential difference in their *objective*.

The similarities however are striking. To begin with, both enterprises have to turn out a variety of products calling for a wide range of skills, and both are so huge that they must adopt a hierarchical structure. The first problem here is how to recruit leaders for the apex of the hierarchy and the second, how to keep them inventive. The Civil Service is torn between those who wish to recruit general ability and train it to specialize, and those who wish to recruit specialists and train them to generalize: so in General Motors.[3] The Civil Service is urged to break down the ivory-tower mentality of its higher grades: General Motors is urged to break down the "parochialism of the executive imagination".[4]

Secondly, since both are enormous and hierarchical, the problem of leadership involves promotion. The Civil Service is sometimes

[1] 692,000 non-industrial, 254,000 industrial: the total payroll for 1946-7 was £592 millions.

[2] Book II.

[3] Drukter, *Big Business*, Heinemann, 1947, pp. 87-9.

[4] Drukter, *op. cit.*, *loc. cit.*

urged to recruit leaders by promotion from within its ranks, sometimes urged to recruit from the outside—and often by the same people.[1] A similar schizophrenia besets General Motors, which hitherto has paralleled the Civil Service in believing it can discover its potential leaders from outside.[2] Both have similar hesitations in their promotion policy, and for the same reason: it is impossible to find an objective criterion of an individual's efficiency. This may seem odd, for private enterprise is said to pay the individual something measured by his marginal productivity. But this is true only of highly competitive small enterprises. In Big Business, each individual contribution to profitability is too small to be measured, and in any case, what relation has profitability to efficiency? This could only be decided if one could perfect *another* yardstick to determine, not only whether the firm is making a profit (which is easy) but also whether that is its maximum possible profit. Such yardsticks are cost accounting and trial and error. General Motors uses both. The O.M. division of the Treasury has been devised for this identical purpose.

Because neither can impute an exact value to any one individual's efficiency, in both the wages and promotion policy tends to be arbitrary. Once profit is made, labour's wage is decided by the higgling of the market. This sets an upward limit on wages in private industry which theoretically does not exist in the Civil Service, and which can only be replaced—as in fact it is—by a policy of organized mean-ness. The Treasury organizes mean-ness admirably.

Finally we meet the hackneyed complaint that Civil Service promotion is slow and often by seniority. It is slow because the vacancies in managerial positions are rare: but so they are in General Motors. The belief that in private industry a capable young man will soon find himself at the top of the tree is true only in competitive industry where he can leave one firm to join another. Inside one huge unit, like General Motors, promotion forms a far more acute grievance than in the Civil Service. It is extremely rare: it is not "based on a clear policy and on any impersonal criterion", and it is the unanimous conviction in the plants that it is based on "rank favouritism, whims and accidents".[3] The British Civil Service with its efficiency sheets and promotion Boards does at least try to give

---

[1] *The Reform of the Higher Civil Service*, Gollancz, 1946.

[2] Drukter, *op. cit.*, pp. 30-32. Both I.C.I. and Unilever recruit by a system similar to the Civil Service Selection Board (the "House Party").

[3] Drukter, *op. cit.*, at pp. 146-7.

an appearance of fairness, and does provide some impersonal kind of appeal.[1]

Such are the similarities. They are striking for they are another aspect of the problem of *size*. Where then does Big Business differ from the Civil Service? The answer is, *in direction*. They have entirely dissimilar objectives. The Civil Service differs from General Motors precisely in that it does not exist to make a profit. Hence its members' incentive is, *in the last resort*,[2] to draw a salary, and not, by taking risks, to make a lot of money. Secondly, it is *public*. Hence its actions are subject to persistent scrutiny and liable to disavowal. This again limits its flexibility and enterprise. Thirdly, while the servants of a big company are, in the last resort responsible to shareholders who rarely meet and are ill-qualified to criticize, Civil Servants and their Ministers must face constant informed criticism from Parliament.This fortifies their unreadiness to take chances. Finally, its services are vital. This forces it to pay especial care to its staff relations, and, in order to prevent disaffection or dispute, to cultivate equality of treatment at the possible expense of quality of service.

II

Up to 1855, the British Civil Service was recruited by personal recommendation. It was manned by spoilsmen for the consolidation of political power, not for efficiency. Upon some more objective test being demanded, the questions arose: first, what kind of test, second what kind of qualification, and third, whether the final arbiter should be the heads of each separate department, or some independent and impartial body. The essential answers given by the nineteenth century govern the Civil Service to this day. The test is open competitive examination or interview, the qualification is general educational ability, the arbiter the Civil Service Commission.

Candidates for the general administrative and clerical posts must compete in a written examination and submit to personal interview. The candidates engaged are those who have the highest aggregate marks. The examination offers a wide choice of subjects based on the curricula of Universities and of the State educational

---

[1] See below. Cf. Appendix to 9th Report, Select Committee on Estimates, 1947-8

[2] But only "in the last resort". The quest for honours, and to get on faster than one's colleagues can sometimes act as a significant goad.

system: it is a test of ability (or teachability) not of knowledge. The papers are set, and marked, by the Civil Service Commission. This body now consists of four members. Its regulations must be approved by the Treasury, but otherwise it is completely independent. Subject to no Minister, and free of partisan pressure by continuous tradition since its birth in 1855, its individual decisions are never questioned.

The Commission exists to assess ability independent of the departments, and at the outset the Permanent Heads strongly resented the way it limited their free choice of personnel. It is not however entirely incompatible with such free choice. It would be possible to place the successful candidates on a waiting list and allow Permanent Heads to pick and choose among them. This is indeed the usual U.S.A. practice, but in England the principle of a single and indivisible service triumphed. This had two corollaries. In the first place, the successful candidate, although encouraged to state the Ministry he prefers, will not necessarily be posted there, and, once posted, is always liable to transfer. Secondly, since the service is not divided by virtue of technical skills, it is divided by virtue of general capabilities. The distinctions are not departmental but hierarchical, i.e. between grade and grade, each common to the whole service. This conception (and all those mentioned so far) originated in the Trevelyan-Northcote Report of 1853, which drew a sharp distinction between "intellectual" work and "mechanical" work. The distinction gave rise to the "Upper and Lower" divisions, subsequently renamed the First and Second, and finally, to the four general divisions in use to-day.

The administrative grade is a policy making, managerial grade, very small and very selective. Its numbers have increased from 1500 (1939) to 4200. The standard of its written recruitment examination is high, viz. 2nd Class Honours. At the moment an additional method of examination is also in use, the so-called "House Party". There is a qualifying examination in English, general paper, and intelligence tests. Those who qualify spend two days at a country house where they are induced to submit to a series of tests of personal qualities. They then attend for a final interview with a Selection Board. This consists of the First Civil Service Commissioner, representatives of the other Commissioners, some Civil Servants, business men, trade unionists and university representatives.[1]

[1] 9th Report, Select Committee on Estimates, 1947–8, Minutes of Evidence, *passim*.

The Executive Grade "are responsible for carrying out policy and for handling individual cases where judgment, initiative and resource" are needed.[1] They have increased from 18,500 (1939) to 50,000. Here the written examination standard is Higher School Certificate or its equivalent.

The Clerical Grade "undertake ordinary clerical duties, such as the handling of straightforward correspondence, checking accounts, preparing statistics, summarizing complicated issues for consideration by senior staff".[2] Its size has risen from 77,000 before the War to 264,000. There is also a very small sub-clerical or typist grade, to be recruited exclusively among women. For both of these classes, the examination standard is School Certificate.

This description must now be qualified. In the first place, it applies only to the *Home* Civil Service; there is also a Scientific Civil Service, a Foreign Service and a Colonial Service. In all three, recruitment is again by competitive examination and interview through the Civil Service Commission but the qualifications differ from the general ones given above. In the second place, inside the Home Civil Service itself there are certain "Departmental" classes, viz. the Inland Revenue Inspectorate, the Special Departmental Class of the Ministry of Labour, the Officers of Customs and Excise. These are recruited through the Civil Service Commission by open competition, but again the qualifications for grading tend to differ from the bulk of the Service. Thirdly there are numbers of scientific, legal, medical men, factory inspectors, accountants, engineers, architects, surveyors and draughtsmen who are recruited by professional qualification and competitive interview.

III

Pay and conditions are generalized over the whole Civil Service according to one's grade and status therein, while office discipline, organization and above all promotion remains a departmental matter. This distinction is utilitarian. Since it is impossible to compute the exact money worth of each officer there is no economic reason why pay should not be generalized. Since it would not only be unfair but unpolitic to pay varying departmental scales to Civil Servants who entered at the same educational level, perform similar work, and are often not in the department of their choice, there is a

[1] Civil Service, Careers Handbooks, Min. of Labour.
[2] *Op. cit.*, p. 5.

very good reason *for* the practice. It results, as a matter of history, from the rankling grievances produced among the staff in 1870-1890 by these very conditions and the staffs' unremitting pressure for equal treatment. As a corollary the reluctant Treasury was made to undertake the task of standardization, in obedience to the Ridley Commission of 1889. Similar pressure from the scientists induced the Treasury to re-classify them into a Scientific Service, after the Second World War.

Further than this the Treasury stubbornly refused to move. It declined to undertake what it believed to be the Ministers' responsibilities either in regard to office organization or to promotion. The pressure put on it resulted as already described, in a division of responsibility between its own Establishment and O.M. departments, and departmental Establishment and O.M. officers. When it deals with pay it must establish a relationship between a classification of the work performed and what it deems an appropriate salary range. This is its official responsibility by the Order in Council of 1920; but in practice it classifies and reclassifies in intimate consultation with the Civil Service Commission, the Departmental Establishment Officers and the staff trade unions.

Promotion is (with the exception of a few of the very highest posts, which are Prime Minister's appointments) a purely departmental matter. For posts under £700 p.a., special precautions are taken to ensure that it is made as objectively as possible. Each Civil Servant has an Annual Report Sheet prepared by his superiors. These are standardized forms, containing a number of headings which relate to knowledge, personality, judgment, zeal and so forth. The superior must endorse each of these as average, above, or below average, and state whether the officer is not fitted for promotion, fitted for promotion, or "eminently fitted". If the Report is adverse, the Civil Servant must see it and sign it.

Ordinary promotions, below the rank of Principal of the Administrative Class, are *ceteris paribus* most largely influenced by seniority, and the lower down the hierarchy the less *ceteris paribus* there is about it. Exceptional promotions, as from one grade to another, naturally receive far closer attention.

The method of selection varies between Departments according to the arrangements made with the staff organizations. Usually a special Board is convened, consisting of the department's Establishment Officer, the head of the branch in which the vacancy has occurred, and usually, another. Sometimes a short list of candidates will be drawn up and the candidates summoned for interview, some-times the Board will recommend to the Head of the Department on the basis of the annual report sheets. The system has gone a long way to meet the suspicions of favouritism and intrigue so rife in industry, and so has an injured officer's right of appeal. Such appeals are direct to the Head of the Department who deals with the case personally, either with or without assessors.

This extreme care to achieve objectivity is but another aspect of the quest for equality of treatment between Civil Servants, and it is striking that the General Secretary of the Civil Service Clerical Association can write: "One of the causes of discontent ... is the differences in promotion opportunities between Departments ... there is an incessant demand from the staff of less fortunate Depart-ments for a "pooling" scheme to equalize promotion chances."[1] It illustrates the caution with which staff relationships must be handled.

To this end, the Civil Service is covered, as a whole and depart-mentally, by a system of Whitley Councils. These, representing the Heads of Departments and the Staffs, deal with such matters as promotion policy, discipline, conditions of work, and office organ-ization. The National Council is largely concerned with more general principles of pay, classification, promotion, education and training. The claims, involving salaries under £700, which cannot be settled here, may be taken to the Arbitration Court. Unfortunately, its great usefulness is limited because claims can only be made for "classes" not individuals, and the Treasury is the sole interpreter of its judgments.

[1] L. C. White, *A Modern Guide to the Civil Service*, University of London Press, 1945.

Chapter 2

THE ADMINISTRATIVE GRADE

"... These unhappy people were proposing Schemes for persuading Monarchs to choose favourites upon the Score of their wisdom, capacity and virtue; of teaching Ministers to consult the publick good; of rewarding merit, Great abilities and Eminent services ... of choosing for employments persons qualified to exercise them; with many other wild impossible chimaeras ..."

Swift: A Voyage to Laputa.

I

THE duties of the Administrative Grade have been authoritatively defined[1] as:

"Those concerned with the *formation of policy*, with the co-ordination and improvement of Government machinery, and with the *general administration* and control of the Departments of the Public Service."

The italicized words sound the keynote. This grade comprises the immediate advisers and entourage of the Minister, and they are not technicians, not even in the most technical Ministry.

Is this wise? Indeed, how can one justify an Administrative Grade at all? Over the last half century the duties of Government have become increasingly technical and scientific; yet the supreme control of departments like the Ministry of Health or the Ministry of Agriculture, and the chief channel of advice to the Minister, is still vested in a Permanent Head who has usually been recruited for ability in classics, history, or mathematics—indeed, in every group of subjects other than the technical details of the department he is supposed to control. Economic departments like the Board of Trade are not governed by businessmen but by academic theorists. Again,

[1] R.C. on Civil Service, Cmd. 3909 of 1931, the "Tomlin Commission", p. 102.

as the historical roots of open competition are re-examined, it appears as an instrument of the middle class, designed to permit their sons who filled the public schools and Universities, to oust the underlings of aristocracy.[1] Whereas—so this argument continues—the limited "police" and supervisory duties of the Victorian State might be adequately served by literati and Brahmins, the modern state needs scientists and businessmen. The criticism sometimes goes so far as to suggest that an Administrative Grade is not necessary, and that departments should be controlled by a Board of technicians.[2] It is impossible therefore to assess the Administrative Grade until the claims of scientists and board management have been discussed.

The scientists have three grievances. First of all, they protested, they were not organized and classified as a group but split into bits and pieces among the departments. This complaint was fully justified. In 1937 there were some 8000 specialists, but they were organized in 120 different hierarchies with over 450 salary scales; they were abominably ill paid also, the highest salary available being £2500 p.a. It took the Second World War, and a permanent rise in their numbers to 37,000 to set this grievance to rights, and to create the Scientific Civil Service with its central recruitment and a few easily recognizable grades and salary scales.

Their remaining two complaints however raised the central problem of their relations to the Administrative Grade. They resented the fact that so few scientists were ever drawn into that grade and so permitted to shape policy.[3] Secondly, they were not prepared to play a merely consultative part. The right of access to the minister did not suffice them, for it was necessary to know when to insist on this right, and this meant knowing what policies were under discussion. In any case, such advice, solicited or unsolicited, *after* policy had been decided elsewhere, was of a mere technical kind; seized with the whole problem the scientist might have provided a completely different and simpler approach. In the first case the scientist is approached to make a better nose cap, tail fin or

[1] Morley, *Life of Gladstone*, Letter to Lord J. Russell, 20 Jan., 1854, in Appendix.

[2] Selby-Bigge, *The Board of Education*, p. 206. Tomlin Commission, para. 176. For an extreme and incautious indictment of the Administrative Grade on these lines, see, for instance, Hamilton, *History of the Homeland*, Allen and Unwin, p. 286.

[3] In 1931 out of 20 posts worth over £3000 p.a. only 2 were filled by scientists.

explosive for an existing bomb: in the second he is told "the problem is to blow up this dam—can you devise a bomb to do it?" A typical complaint is put thus, by a former Chief Medical Officer of the Local Government Board.[1]

"there was honest belief ... that technical advice is advice which is not to be given until called for by the Secretariat who, it is assumed, are entirely competent to decide whether such advice is needed.

"Second, when such advice is on record it is assumed that it can safely be re-applied in what are regarded by the Secretariat as analogous circumstances. ... When technical advice has been given and is on the 'minutes', there is the further occasional great defect that ...

"Third, the Secretary of the Department, in major instances its Minister, may decide contrary to expert advice without having heard personally the statements and arguments of the expert advisers—"[2]

Neither complaint has been met. It was justly pointed out that a scientific officer must have administrative capacity before being called into the Administrative Grade; but Permanent Heads seem to have shown no marked haste to rush out and test it. As to the status and role of scientific advisers, the demands could be met fully only if departmental heads were replaced by Boards on which the technical and scientific officers would sit as of right. Except in the G.P.O., this proposal has been discountenanced throughout the Civil Service, and rightly. A Board cannot do any of the three things a Permanent Head is supposed to do, i.e. focus issues for his Minister, lead his Department, and individualize responsibility. It is significant that the U.S.A. should turn its back so decisively on Board management, after so long an experience of it. It is characterized as "slow, cumbersome, wasteful and ineffective", tending to "diffuse responsibility, to produce delays and to make effective co-operation or vigorous leadership impossible—"[3]

---

[1] Sir Arthur Newsholme, *Last 30 Years in Public Health*, Allen and Unwin, 1936, pp. 62-3.

[2] Cf. also Tomlin Commission, para. 174-5.

[3] President's Committee on Administrative Management, p. 10. Compare Sir Charles Reid's remark on the National Coal Board, after his resignation: "The vital changes necessary to make the organization effective and efficient, can only be carried out by a strong policy board whose members are divorced from functional duties".

The fashion for creating Semi-Public Corporations does not dispose of these arguments. True, they are usually run by technical boards, without any Administrative Grade. Yet Ministries differ from them profoundly, and the particular wherein they differ is precisely that which makes an Administrative Grade necessary. These corporations have a cut-and-dried task—to raise coal, generate gas and electricity, run trains and administer docks. This is broadly an exercise in quantities not "quality"—and it is significant that in making non-technical, i.e. policy decisions, not the Board is responsible but the Minister. Secondly their finances are autonomous; this is working capital for which they are not accountable to the Treasury unless they become insolvent. Finally their day-to-day administration is autonomous. A Ministry differs in that in every one of these matters it is *answerable*. Its work is not primarily technical but involves public policy, i.e. qualitative decisions. They are qualitative in that they must strike a mean between what the service requires and can do, and what the public will not stand. Its task is to execute public will and in this it is subject to day-to-day cross examination by its masters, the M.P.s. A Minister's first task is not to provide the technically best solution but to satisfy Parliament. If the two go together, so much the better for both. If otherwise, not technique must be courted but Parliament.

The Minister cannot do this without the Administrative Grade, whose first duty is to concentrate the issues of the department in such a way that his decision is not ill-informed and rapidly formed. It is not enough for his advisers to tell him what his own department is working on, and what problems are likely to arise. They must also advise him what policy is palatable to the other ministries, what Parliamentary interests are likely to oppose it and which is the best political strategy to adopt. They must temper their appreciation of technical beauty with a keen sense of their public relations. In short the Administrative Grade and its hierarchical form is necessary precisely because the work of a ministry demands a sense of public policy as well as a grasp of techniques. This may seem absolutely regrettable. It is always sad when ideals surrender to expediency.

II

So much depends on the quality of the Administrative Grade that every effort must be made to improve it. Yet some criticisms seem excessively unfair. It should not be reproached, for instance, because the majority of its members are drawn from the older Universities. This reflects inequalities in the educational system and the remedy lies there. Again there is a perennial whine that civil servants are timid, formal, verbose and dull. In his *Civil Service in the Changing State*, Mr Greaves has collected together a whole mass of such depressing charges, and after making due allowance he concludes:

"there must be a clear cut policy of testing men for inventiveness, of seeking and rewarding initiative ... of looking out for the man who shows original thought."[1]

Now either this says too little or too much. It says too little in the sense that I would look for similar qualities if I had to change my grocer. If it is qualified, as it is, by the remark "whether that originality be wholly acceptable or not", and that "great administrators have always been men who have known when it was more important to do the required thing than to avoid giving offence", then it might very well go much too far. The civil servant is at worst an adviser and at best a *locum tremens*. The qualities demanded by such critics of the Civil Service are far more appropriate to the Ministers than to their minions. The civil servant makes policy, only to the extent that he influences his Minister, and the Minister only to the extent that *he* influences Parliament. Of ourse it is true that our great administrators have been

Impiger, iracundus, inexorabilis, acer.

Such were the Chadwicks, the Trevelyans, the Stephens and the Morants. They nagged and drove and beat this country along the road of social progress, and everybody remembers them with *reminiscent* gratitude—after they are dead—but what Cabinet would want a Service alive and bursting with them?

The difficulty is that "Virtue itself hath need of limits" and the limits to the Permanent Head's official virtue change arbitrarily. It is all very fine and large to construct the catalogue of virtues: philosophers have been at it ever since Plato wrote the *Republic* and Xenophon the *Cyropaedia*. The questions are—in what degree? How will you test for that degree? How will you keep it to that degree? And here there seems to be a general consensus that the Administrative Grade might be improved by amendments along lines which include the methods of recruitment, post entry training,

[1] *Op. cit.*, p. 67.

central promotion, and dismissal. Even so a caution is necessary. No objective criterion is available to determine whether or not the service really has improved. The only proof of the pudding is in the eating, but in this instance the eaters are an ever changing queue 50 million strong. ...

Two methods of recruitment are now in force for the Home Civil Service: 75 per cent of the vacancies are filled by the competitive written examination, the remainder by the Civil Service Selection Board (or "House Party"). Their respective merits have been widely canvassed and disputed. Yet they cannot differ widely either in academic standard or in fairness. Although "written", the competitive examination awards 300 out of 1300 marks on interview and this plays a decisive role; although based on interview, the House Party method demands 2nd Class Honours as its qualifying standard. As for fairness, after all, the candidate may choose the method he prefers. The real question is—which system recruits the better civil servant? But what is a "better" civil servant? Attempts to show that candidates recruited by one method were subsequently promoted more rapidly than candidates recruited by the other are misleading, since the factors affecting promotion in each case may not be uniform. The present practice of collating elaborate "follow-through" reports on the candidates may after some years provide the materials for a reasoned choice between the two systems.[1]

A less personal answer might be returned however to that other problem of recruitment—whether entrants should be brought in from the professions and industry. Against it, "old hands" argue that such people would be those who had "failed in life", that they would offend the career civil servants, whose promotion they had blocked, that they would be too old for the initial two or three years' drudgery, or too young for responsibility. Personal acquaintance with many able academics who gave up their University positions for what proved to be brilliant careers in the public service convinces me that the first objection is sheer nonsense. As to the others the éclat with which the newcomers to the service carried out their work during the Second World War, and the noticeable impoverishment of the service after they had left it, would itself provide an answer. Even in 1939, out of 80 higher posts investigated, no less than 14 were "outside" appointees as against 45 who had

[1] See the 9th Report of the Select Committee of Estimates, 1947–48. This is a highly important document.

entered in the usual way.[1] But the need is to-day far greater than in the pre-war period. With its extended economic functions, for instance, the service demands not only those who would make good "managers"—these are the types it trains—but also men who have contacts, knowledge of markets, and how to carry through decisions in these hitherto unfamiliar fields. If the State is going into Big Business it must pick a proportion of its leaders as Big Business does —from small competitive business: and for the same reason. And what is more, the salaries of the higher Civil Service, wretchedly low compared with private enterprise, will have to be raised sharply.[2]

A third and related problem turns on the proportion of recruits to be drawn from the Executive Grade. Until 1914 the "promotion barrier" was almost unsurmountable, but under pressure from the staff side it was lowered gradually, until in 1931 the Tomlin Commission reported that 25 per cent of the Administrative Grade, had been promoted to it from other grades, and that, of the 20 highest posts, 2 had been filled by officers so promoted. The tradition has recently been formalized by the Treasury's decision to fill 20 per cent of all Assistant Principalships by a "limited competition" examination open to the whole service outside the Administrative Grade.[3]

Post-entry training could be very much improved. It has never been systematic—the newcomer "learned by doing"; and to-day his superiors are too harassed and overworked to allow him to do even that. Yet such training is a logical corollary of recruitment by general examination. The Treasury has arranged a 3-weekly course for newcomers but the time is miserably insufficient and one could hardly say that the course is taken to heart. One answer might well be a more formalized and systematic "learning by doing" than is, unfortunately, possible at the moment. In addition all commentators agree that the Principal who is about to become an Assistant Secretary should be granted sabbatical leave and spend it abroad or on interchange with local government or industry.

Although the promotion system has never been seriously attacked, inside the Administrative Grade, bearing most hardly as it does inside the lower Grades, a serious issue is whether promotions, like recruitments, should be centralized. The Departmental staff resent

[1] *The Reform of the Higher Civil Service*, Gollancz, 1947, p. 45.

[2] This is now accepted officially, and salaries are to be raised gradually. Cf. Cmd. 7635, Chorley Committee on *Higher Civil Service Remuneration* (February, 1949).

[3] *Reform of the Higher Civil Service*, Fabian Society, Gollancz, 1947.

newcomers from other departments and argue that they would waste a good deal of time settling down to learn a new routine. But most educators agree that when a school needs a new headmaster nothing succeeds so well as an outsider. Furthermore, pooled promotions, by increasing the amount of cross posting, would correct a very serious defect of the service, namely that the high prestige departments like the Treasury and Home Office tend to get first pick of recruits, since these naturally put them down as the departments of their first choice. Thus like attracts like, the "better" departments stay better and the worse, worse. An identical situation led, until the Ministry of Education tried to correct it, to the older Universities "creaming" the best of the State Scholars. Finally the field would be far wider and so the quality of the higher Civil Service progressively better. As for resentment, it would die away if the practice became universal and common form.

Lastly there is the question of dismissal. Although every successful entrant must serve a probation period before being fully established, it is rare to have him dismissed, and once established almost never dismissed.[1] It is admitted on all sides that the Service ought to be able to dismiss its incompetents and misfits instead of finding them a simpler job to do, yet the proposal has been held up by a dispute between the staff side of the Whitley Council, and the Treasury. The Treasury are prepared to retire men, as the Foreign Service does, with their proportionate pensions plus a sum going up to £100 p.a. as compensation. The staff side refuse to accept this for the Home Service unless the Treasury also concede the right to voluntary retirement with full pension rights. This the Treasury declines because it would make it very easy for certain staffs with special knowledge (e.g. of factory inspection)—to retire and use their knowledge in private enterprises. It also objected that technicians, trained in the Service, would tend to slip away into private industry. Agreement is surely practicable, possibly by banning such private employment for a set number of years, as a prior condition to entering the Service.[2]

[1] All "doubtful" probationers are re-examined by a Central Probation Board. This consists of the 1st Civil Service Commissioner, the Head of the Department concerned, the Head of another Department, and one other member.

[2] In December 1948, it was announced that a bill would be brought forward to enable a Civil Servant to retire voluntarily with his accrued pension rights at the age of 50: while the Departments will be able to sack a man "in the interests of efficiency", and pay him only his *proportionate* pension.

These are by no means the only methods suggested for improving the Administrative Grade but they are the major ones. The root of the difficulty is still there however: even if all these devices are adopted, there is still no yardstick by which any improvement can be measured, and no means so far by which any observed improvements in particular respects can be correlated with any one of these devices. In the last resort the test at present is what Parliament thinks of the quality of administration and what its special committees are able to find out. This leads directly to the accountability of the Civil Servant, the subject of the next and concluding Book.

THE LOCAL GOVERNMENT SERVICE

"They are always employed in some business except in the times of eating and sleeping, which are very short."

Swift: A Voyage to Lilliput.

THE national Civil Service is not the only body of public servants to feel the effects of the Administrative Revolution. This has sharply affected the personnel practices of what are, increasingly, the quasi-agents of the central Departments, viz. the Local Authorities. These now employ some 1,300,000 persons—an increase of nearly 400,000 on 1939! Leaving aside the teachers (173,000), and the Police, Firemen and Civil Defence workers (88,000), the remainder comprises about one million manual workers (of whom nearly one fifth are occupied in the local trading services) and about 130,000 professionals, general administrators and clerical assistants, of whom about 9000 are technical and professional appointments.

These proportions strike the sharpest contrast to the national Civil Service and illustrate the degree to which the local authorities are executive bodies, while the majority of the central departments are still regulatory and promotional. It is the body of 130,000 technicians and administrators that alone invites comparison with the national Civil Service. Here the new demands of public administration have been put so urgently that what before the Second World War was a shapeless and characterless collection of exclusively local staffs is now adapting to its own use the leading features of central Civil Service practice and turning itself into a national and unitary Local Government Service.

Until 1946 such a term was a misnomer. There was not one service, but several. Except for the few Statutory appointments and qualifications each authority was as completely autonomous in all staff matters as any private firm. First, each authority was its own paymaster and so, whereas among the Ministries the Treasury, as common paymaster can formulate grades and salary scales common to them all, there was among the Authorities no national standard of classification and pay; each established its own system. Again, whereas the uniformity of classification enables the Civil Service Commission, an impartial outside authority, to devise appropriate and uniform tests for recruiting to each grade, the local service recognized neither national standards for recruitment nor any central body to apply them. Finally while transfer of personnel from one ministry to another is physically simple, transfer between Authorities meets the obstacle of *space*. Only the higher officers tend to transfer; 95 per cent of the local staffs are locally recruited and locally rooted.

So personnel policies varied enormously between authorities. This was partly due to the wide divergencies in their size, and consequently in their needs. It was also due to their loose internal organization, for no authorities possess a single committee or department which combines, as the Treasury does, the control of finance and the budget, the classification and pay of the staffs, and a share in recruitment policy. Instead local budgets were controlled by the Finance Committee, and recruitment was divided between the Permanent Heads of Departments (for minor appointments), the employing Committee (for the more important ones), and, for the heads of departments, the Council itself. Establishment committees did not always exist. Those that did differed widely among themselves, for while some dealt with all matters affecting staff, others merely prescribed general conditions of service and gave general directions on employment policy to the employing committees who were left free to apply them to particular cases.

Recruitment was haphazard. It worked most successfully when the appointments demanded professional or technical qualifications. Here the professional associations had themselves already set up nationally recognized standards. It worked very badly in the appointment of clerical or administrative officers. The L.C.C. with its 80,000 officers could afford to recruit by competitive examination for 18 year old entrants, a few of the larger authorities recruited this way for 15 and 16 year old entrants; the others were much too small. Recruits would be admitted at varying ages, and their educational qualifications would vary not only between one authority and another but even between the various departments of one particular authority. Some authorities advertised their vacancies, others had private arrangements with local schoolmasters, still others had no set system at all. The evidence shows that in the smaller authorities patronage and corruption were by no means unknown.

Again, although since 1929 the Ministry of Health had tried to get the authorities to adopt specific scales of salaries and to institute classification systems, 1939 saw scores of authorities which had neither. In such circumstances it was Utopian to talk of those "broadly similar staff grades in force throughout the local government service" without which the movement of officers between authorities was seriously restricted and their ladder of promotion confined exclusively to one area. Moreover promotion methods were not only not uniform between authorities but were quite haphazard in all but the very largest. These few did maintain efficiency ratings like the national Civil Service. The majority however kept no records at all and promotion policy appeared arbitrary. Furthermore since the local officer, whether clerk or Department Head, is liable[1] to dismissal at the Council's pleasure, he might have small chance of redress or even of appeal. There is no doubt that in some councils the elected representatives abused the power which their authority thus gave them.

The inter-war period saw a mounting pressure for a "single" "national" service, that is for nationally accepted standards in grading, pay and recruitment, and nationally accepted systems of promotion and training. The staffs demanded it in the name of equal treatment, fair promotions, secure tenure, and a nation-wide field for promotion. in short to improve their own career prospects. The Onslow Commission of 1929 and the Hadow Committee (1934) stressed in addition the inefficiency and waste of the existing lack of system. The methods of recruitment were alleged to be "at least open to question"[2] and the lack of a considered policy as "short-sighted and wasteful".[3] Nevertheless the extent to which the local service could be made to conform to Civil Service practice is limited. The difference between the two are not the outcome simply of parochialism and obstinacy on the part of local councillors. The two services differ inherently by reason of three factors. First they differ in object, and therefore composition. Secondly, the principle of differentiation is in the one by functional departments and in the other by territorial areas. Thirdly, the Civil Service enjoys all the

[1] Except where Ministerial consent is needed.

[2] Royal Commission on Local Government, Final Report (Cmd. 3436), p. 128.

[3] Report to the Minister of Health on ... Local Government Officers. (Hadow Report), p. 4.

advantages of bigness, while the local service contains a multitude of lilliputian staffs.

The object of the Local Government Service is far more strictly executive than the Civil Service and hence only one tenth of its numbers are in a position truly comparable to the 750,000 non-industrial staff of the Ministries. The staff relations of its million manual workers are already looked after by the Trade Unions. Furthermore whereas the reform of the central Civil Service began with the need for better *leadership*, i.e. from the reform of the Administrative Grade, and then extended downwards and outwards through the whole service, this could not be true of the local Government Service. There, the problem of leadership was already solved. The top appointments are not administrative but professional or technical, for the Committee structure of local councils makes an administrative grade unnecessary. The leadership in the local government service is therefore recruited by reference to their diplomas and previous experience with other authorities, and there exists for them a real ladder of promotion by transfer from one authority to another. In fact their conditions approximate to the technician in private industry. Since then good heads of departments could be secured in this way, while the Unions looked after the interests of the manual workers, the impulse to reform the local government service has largely sprung from and confined itself to the persons who in the central Civil Service would comprise the Executive and Clerical classes; and these are not only a mere fraction of the mass but they are split up among 1500 separate employers.

This territorial dispersion does not only mean that they are more difficult to organize and combine than the central staffs. Collective bargaining implies a common front on both sides, and, because they are organized upon a *territorial* basis, the local authorities are far less inter-dependent than the central departments, organized as these are upon a *functional* basis. Consequently whereas the Treasury can integrate the staff practices of separate Ministries, an equivalent for the local authorities could only be one of two things—either a national system imposed by the Central Government or voluntary agreement between the authorities. The first is politically most undesirable. It is precisely because in France the teachers, police and local officials are appointed by and dismissible by the central government that the Executive enjoys its formidable powers and opportunities to intervene in the electoral process and subvert the free expression of popular will. This is hardly possible in Great Britain where the secrecy of the ballot, the maintenance of order, and the electoral influence of the public service is distributed and scattered among 15,000 jealous local authorities which in these respects are almost totally independent of the Cabinet. The alternative then was a voluntary agreement; and this had to meet the same kind of obstacles that all other voluntary agreements of local authorities encounter. The richer and larger had good systems of their own, could pay high salaries and attract competent staffs. The poorer declined to bind themselves to paying higher wages and regretted surrendering their patronage.

The Civil Service and the Local Government Service must differ finally, because of the factor of *size*. The Civil Service finds classification or efficiency ratings both necessary and practicable because it deals with large numbers.

"A large authority may require several hundreds of officers; a small one perhaps not more than ten ... Officers bearing the same titles may have very different responsibilities according to the functions of their respective authorities. Methods of recruitment which may be desirable in the larger offices may not be practicable where few officers are employed. The small authorities necessarily offer a more limited prospect than the medium sized and large; they can allow little specialization; in many cases they cannot afford to employ the whole time services of professional officers."[1]

Consequently any approach to standardizing conditions must fall short of the practice of the Civil Service. It must confine itself to constructing a much more general framework within which the authorities would play a considerably more independent role than the Ministries do in establishing their schemes of staff conditions. This is realized by the *Scheme of Service* which the staff Unions,[2] after two decades of pressure, finally succeeded in negotiating with the various authorities in 1945. The Scheme uses as its instruments the Provincial Joint Councils first set up after the First World War and which comprise representatives of the staff and of the authorities. Up to 1939 only three such councils functioned. The Second World War created an atmosphere favourable to the completion of the chain of nine. After these had been set up the edifice was crowned by the establishment of a National Council in 1945 and

[1] Hadow Committee Report, p. 120.
[2] Notably The National Association of Local Government Officers (N.A.L.G.O.)

with it the negotiation of the "National Scheme". It is open to any Local authority to decline to recognize the scheme; but since it is the product of the National Council it embodies the joint agreement of both staffs' and employers' associations, and both sides recommend their clientèle to accept it. At the moment of writing only 50 out of the 1550 authorities have refused. In this way the haphazard and formless heap of local personnel policies has been transformed into something like a single uniform service and most of the Hadow Committee's proposals at last put into effect.

The scheme represents a remarkably workmanlike compromise between the legitimate needs of the individual councils in their capacity of employers, and the conception of the service as national and unitary.

It applies to all officers earning under £700 per annum. These are to be recruited at the age of 16 and if admitted are subject to 6 months probation. In some cases officers may be recruited at the age of 18. All 16 year old candidates must pass a dual test, a qualifying examination of not lower than School Certificate standard followed by competitive examination and interview. For the 18 year old candidates admission is by the second test only. All this represents the *national* framework. Within it the examination itself remains to be arranged by the Local Authority or the Provincial Joint Council. Similarly with post-entry training; Authorities are to give their officers facilities for study, and encourage them to read for University Degrees, the Diploma of Public Administration, or professional qualifications. The schemes themselves however are a matter either for the Joint Council or for negotiations between the Local Authority's Establishment Committee and Staff Representatives.

A similar duality is discernible in the classification scheme. The whole service is divided into 5 grades: the General, the Clerical, the Higher Clerical, the Miscellaneous and the Administrative Professional and Technical Division. Appropriate salary scales for each are laid down on a national basis. This represents a set of national categories—but it is left to the individual authority to decide which officers it shall fit into which categories. Here the Provincial Joint Council has been given jurisdiction over appeals, while the National Council is trying to formulate hard and fast descriptions which could apply automatically in all authorities.

Finally the scheme enjoins certain important safeguards of the local officers' prospects. Provision is made to prevent canvassing and soliciting councillors, and to check nepotism, while the pro-

131

motion system is to embody an Annual Report Sheet system akin to that of the Civil Service. These sheets are to be used as the basis of promotion. Furthermore there is an efficiency bar to recruits who have entered at the lowest grade, viz. the General Division. To rise further they must have passed a qualifying examination, professional or general. The degrees or diplomas which will be accepted are specified in the Scheme and the National Council has also sponsored its own general qualifying examination and its own examination system.

The transformation is remarkable. At a stroke system has replaced a chaos. Furthermore it represents perhaps the most striking case of local self-help in the last fifty years of local government history. The next step is for authorities to set up their own efficiency auditors whose task it would be to carry out surveys of the relative efficiency of local services in comparable areas, i.e. the local equivalent of the O.M. division of the Treasury. The "Scheme" has opened a way for greatly improving the calibre of local government staffs. There still remains this task of devising machinery to test the degree of the improvements and perfecting organization and methods to use the staffs to best advantage.

BOOK V

CHAPTER 1

THE DILEMMAS OF PUBLIC ACCOUNTABILITY

"This illustrious person had very usefully employed his studies in finding out effectual Remedies for all diseases and corruptions to which the several kinds of publick Administration are subject by the Vices or infirmities of those who govern as well as by the Licentiousness of those who are to obey—"

Swift: A Voyage to Laputa.

SCRIPTURE enjoins us to forgive them that trespass against us; but not when they are civil servants. On the contrary! Western constitutionalism has been one sustained effort to simplify pursuit and popularize penalties. The administrator is *accountable* for his actions; and accountable moreover, not to his own stricken conscience, but to the *public*. There were no constitutional guarantees against the Guardians, in Plato's Republic: properly bred, they would automatically be "gentle to their fellows and fierce to their enemies".[1] Western democracy has declined to be so trustful, holding with Theodore Roosevelt that "if you give a man power to do right you also give him the power to do wrong." And it has devoted itself to elaborating means to prevent wrong, or redress it.

The problem has arisen partly because of the great size of the modern state which divorces the men who take day to day decisions from the masses, and partly because of its complexity which demands that the execution of such decision be entrusted to skilled professionals. The easiest way of solving the problem would be by self administration, everyone participating directly in making decisions and executing them, like an Icelandic Thing,[2] democratic Athens,[3] or the village communities of modern Anarchism. This is to-day impossible. Yet the idea dies hard. It underlay Andrew Jackson's spoils system, the "rotation of office",[4] and Lenin's similar doctrines

[1] II, 375.
[2] Bryce, *Studies in the History of Jurisprudence*, Vol. II, Essay v.
[3] Eyre, *History of Europe*, Vol. 1; (Gomme, *Greek City State*.)
[4] White. *Public Administration*, Macmillan, 1947, p. 280.

in the *State and Revolution*.[1] Both believed that the ordinary citizen was capable of becoming a civil servant at a moment's notice. Lenin talked of their "simple functions of 'managers' and bookkeepers ... which are now already within the capacity of the average city dweller ... .",[2] and Jackson "believed the duties of all public officers are or at least admit of being made so plain and simple that men of intelligence may readily qualify themselves for their performance."[3] Neither doctrine stood up very long to the increasing technical and professional duties of the modern state. An inefficient and corrupt Civil Service in the U.S.A. was slowly transformed from 1883 into a professional corps of qualified specialists. In the U.S.S.R., self administration gave way to a bureaucracy checked by a "Workers and Peasants Inspection" until this in its turn was discovered to be too amateurish, and was replaced by a professional and permanent "control commission" of the Communist Party,[4] together with a "Ministry of State Control".

The Western evolution met the challenges of size and complexity by Representative Government and Bureaucracy. It has vested public will in an elected legislature and public administration in a corps of paid skilled professionals. Two pyramids of responsibility are created. The one, consisting of skilled administrators, transmits its orders from higher rank to lower. The other consisting of citizens transmits its orders from base to apex. The apices are formed by Parliament and Cabinet. Thus the duties of the Civil Service are defined and limited by a formal expression of public will, i.e. a law, and the performance of those duties, whether non-feasance, malfeasance, or even "super" feasance are judged by reference to the express terms of that law. Accountability is *not* personal, *not* a matter of inner conscience. It is specific, towards those who formulate the public will, or law, or to those who interpret it; that is, to Parliament, or the Courts.

"The law, the whole law and nothing but the law": this expresses the entire duty of the Civil Service. Anything else is punishable.

This leads to the first dilemma of accountability. The power to do wrong is also a power to do right. To limit the one, is to limit the other. By insisting on a strict legality, therefore, one keeps the civil

[1] Little Lenin Library, p. 39. (Lawrence & Wishart.)
[2] *Ibid.*
[3] White, *op. cit., loc. cit.* Cf. J. Swift (Nonesuch Edition) p. 55.
[4] Stalin, *Leninism*, p. 534, also J. Towster, *Political Power in the U.S.S.R.*, pp. 172–5.

servant *up* to the mark but also *down* to the mark. If slackness is punishable, so also is zeal. Legality and initiative make bad bed-fellows. Yet,[1] the last half century has seen the central government take over enterprises formerly voluntary, private or local, all of which were accountable, and all of which likewise possessed special techniques, aptitudes, knowledges and incentives! The Civil Servant who has been bidden to supersede these authorities, is faced with a dilemma: not to show zeal, initiative and imagination is "soulless bureaucracy", and to show them is arbitrary, i.e. illegal, interference!

Consequently, the Parliamentary responsibility of the Minister for his department solves one question only to create another. Theoretically he is responsible for every act of every one of his officials. Since there are 32 Ministers and over half a million officials, this is responsibility in a very Pickwickian sense. Yet Parliament may insist on its reality. In these circumstances, the department must present the least target for attack and play safe at all costs. H.Q. will insist that the regions consult it before they take any action; all decisions will be recorded in writing, and nothing will be done for which there is no precedent. Routine, red tape, and writing supplant ingenuity and innovation. The stricter the accountability the tighter becomes routine. To escape from this dilemma the last thirty years created the so-called Semi Public corporation, and the "independent" board. The service is detached from Parliamentary accountability or local accountability. An apparatus of complaint and redress is set up within the service itself, which takes on a kind of judicial status.

The choice of services to be treated in this way has been determined by two considerations. In both, it is alleged, administration will suffer by too strict a Parliamentary accountability, the first because unsavoury "political" considerations will warp its rectitude, the second because its technical nature demands spontaneity and risk-taking. Public Assistance offers an example of the first type. In 1934 the U.A.B. was set up to supplant the local authorities which had hitherto administered Transitional Benefit and Public Assistance to the able-bodied unemployed. The Board members were not to sit in Parliament. Its negotiations had to be approved by Parliament but once approved it was free of further questioning and interference, while Parliament was expressly forbidden to query its treatment of individual cases. The local authorities were supplanted

---

[1] See Book I, Chapter 1.

by the Boards' own officers. In this way parliamentary and local criticism of its activities was effectively stifled. Henceforth complaints were dealt with by the internal processes of the Board. The individual's benefit rates were settled in the first instance by the local officer: a complainant could appeal from him to a Tribunal, consisting of a Chairman appointed by the Minister of Labour, and a workman representative and one other, both appointed by the Board. This Tribunal's decision was final.

The British Electricity Authority offers an example of the second, or technical type. It is subject to the "long term" control of the Ministry of Fuel and Power, but not to day-to-day control which is protected from Parliamentary questioning, debate and control; the Minister is simply not answerable for such details. This is to allow the fullest flexibility and initiative to the Board who are required to run the industry with at least as great a success as private enterprise. Here again, an internal process of the Authority is designed to take care of consumers' complaints. Each region has its consumers' council to which complaints are made, and the Area Boards of the authority must consult such councils as well as the Central Board before making decisions for their areas.[1] The National Coal Board, a similarly constituted public monopoly also has its consumers' councils.[2]

This solution has not gone unchallenged, either by the Legislature or the Courts. Parliament is very conscious of itself as the sovereign authority of the realm. It denies that any agency can be accountable, if it need not reply to Parliamentary questions.[3]

If appeal to one's M.P. is thus eliminated, so is appeal to the Courts. The Tribunals of the U.A.B., the Consumers' councils of the nationalized industries are themselves courts. But they are tribunals of a peculiar kind, for they are composed of active administrators. No law is so strictly worded as to admit no doubt as to its meaning: all laws confer some discretion on the administrator. Hitherto, a citizen could take the dispute to a court, and get the judges to exercise that discretion, by interpreting the law to fit the particular case, and leaving to the Civil Servant the purely mechanical task of executing their interpretation. The constitution of the

[1] Hansard 24 June 1947, col. 279 *et seq.*
[2] See above, Book III, Chapter 1.
[3] This question much exercised the Commons in 1948. See Hansard, 3 March 1948. The debates merely confirmed the arguments described above.

administrative tribunal excludes the jurisdiction of the courts; the active administrator himself exercises the discretion inherent in the Statute.

Should they do so? The Courts insist that they take a "strict" view, an "impartial" view, that they "apply the law". The administrative tribunals twist these into terms of contempt; "strictness" they contrast with their own "flexibility"; "applying the *Law*" they stigmatize as "legalistic". The dispute really derives from two quite distinct types of procedure. The court itself fetters its own freedom to interpret the law; the administrative tribunal need not. This is the heart of the matter. The judicial process is "stricter" because the Court is bound by a procedure which it cannot alter, by well known rules of construction involving the use of analogous cases where none apply exactly, by *stare decisis* which binds it to accept the rulings of superior courts as actual law, and by the search for precedents. The administrative tribunal is "flexible" because it can adopt and change a procedure to suit itself, it can qualify rules of construction by a knowledge of the general policy of its department, it can reverse and re-reverse its former decisions in accordance with any changes in such policy. The court of law is not interested in the result; the administrative tribunal must be. It is in these senses then that one must understand the distinctions drawn between applying law and applying policy, between strictness and flexibility, impartiality and partisanship.

The prime distinction is that in a purely judicial case the court applies the "law of the land" because there is one to apply. There is a set of laws, rulings and precedents sufficient, *when eked out by construction and analogous cases* to apply to any dispute arising. In an administrative matter, let us say the granting of a road traffic licence, the circumstances on which the licence depends are so various, incommensurable, particular to time and place that the issue is simply, "what is expedient in these circumstances having regard to the public interest as understood by my Department?" The lawyer regards this as entirely arbitrary. The administrator denies that a judge could possibly have the special knowledge of road traffic problems and departmental policy to render a sensible judgment. Perhaps an anecdote provides the best example of these different attitudes. In 1948 the State of Nevada bombarded clouds with dry ice, to bring about a snowfall and thus assist its tourist traffic. The neighbouring State of Utah threatened to bring suit, alleging that those clouds were *its* clouds, and would normally come down in rain over its wheatfields. It seemed to me quite impossible to fight a legal case on such an unprecedented matter. Could one envisage "Federal Clouds Commission" at Washington, allotting clouds to various States in accordance with their respective economic needs? A lawyer's view was as follows: The law forbids you to extract water from a watercourse to the detriment of those who have a right of user. It permits you however to bore a well some distance away, and collect water from underground sources, even if this has the ultimate result of taking from the fixed water course more water than direct extraction. "It all depends," he said, "on whether these clouds pursue an undeviating course from one State to another. If they do they resemble a water course, if they do not, they resemble underground sources." Such diametrically opposed conceptions of how to answer a specific case lie at the source of the dispute between lawyers and administrators. The administrators call the courts expensive, slow, legalistic, they claim that they decide on exceptions and not on classes of cases. They pretend that their training is unsuitable. The lawyer replies that the administrative tribunal uses an unfair procedure and is self interested in the cases coming before it.

The public accountability of the Civil Servant may therefore temper administrative efficiency, either by subjecting it to too minute a parliamentary supervision or too legalistic an interpretation in court. The new services undertaken by the central government demand from the administrator a spontaneity and initiative which such accountability may sterilize. Hence the new devices of the independent board and administrative tribunal. Nevertheless the Commons and the Courts still remain the paramount guarantors of the citizen's rights, and must be further examined.

CHAPTER 2

PARLIAMENTARY CONTROL OF ADMINISTRATION

"He likewise directed that every Senator in the great council of a nation, after he had delivered his opinion and argued in the defence of it, should be obliged to give his vote directly contrary: because if that were done, the Result would infallibly terminate in the Good of the Publick ..."

Swift: A Voyage to Laputa.

THE Commons' control of administration is an incident in its general control of policy. Speaking very generally indeed, in Great Britain policy is held to be decided by how the voting went at the last election and how the Cabinet thinks it is going to go at the next. The control exerted by the Commons is a day-to-day continuous surveillance of *detail*.

The general characteristics of its control spring, as already shown,[1] from the nature of the Cabinet and the party structure. While no government is now defeatable in the House it may easily lose an election. Hence control by the House is effective only to the degree that it mobilizes an outside opinion hostile to the Cabinet's policy or administration, and the measure of its effectiveness is the degree to which forebodings about the next election frighten the government into making a *voluntary* withdrawal. The very strength of the Government in the Commons exacts from it the moral obligation to act as an Aunt Sally. Yet there is always the possibility that the most trivial incident may raise such a storm as to cause the party to appeal to the country, and fight a new election: each petty case of personal maladministration is thus invested with enormous potential significance. With these qualifications, the nature of control is distinguished by its range, from broad departmental policy to minute particular items, by its immediacy, every item being challengeable as and when it arises, by its persistency, for it can be raised as often as the Opposition likes and by its searchingness: the House may not know the truth but it infallibly knows a liar.

The forms of control have been modified by the changing role of

[1] Book I, Chapter 3.

the Commons. In the last 40 years the volume of legislation has risen 2¾ times,[1] but roughly the same amount of time has been spent on it;[2] and it takes up the same proportion, i.e. not quite half, of the total time available.[3] The House has managed to achieve this only by greatly increasing ministerial policy-making and discretion. As the House delegates its law-making functions to the Civil Service, so, however, it feels bound to increase its opportunities for controlling the exercise of such delegation.

Out of 145.4 days (the average length of the sessions between 1906 and 1938) the House employed 15 in the Budget resolutions and Finance Bill, 58.5 in "control and formulation of policy", and 71.9 in legislation. Of this no less than 31 per cent was "opposition time", described by the Clerk of the House as meaning "the right to initiate debate, i.e. choose the subject to be debated, or certain kinds of business taken in what is normally Government time".[4] This excludes question hours, and "private members" time taken up in adjournment motions etc. It relates only to matters chosen for debate by the Opposition front bench.

The chief occasions for criticism are first the set of full dress debates initiated on the King's Speech, substantive motions and Supply days: next the various adjournment debates: and, finally question time. In addition the House has a special apparatus of control over delegated legislation, and also, to some extent, by its Select Committee on Estimates, over departmental practice.

The cardinal instrument for controlling the details of administration is question time. It is the hour which always precedes business on the first four days of the week. The M.P. gives notice by handing his question to the Speaker's Desk. The privilege is so popular that the number of questions that may be asked by one member in any day, has fallen from 8 in 1909 to 4 in 1919 and is now 3. He marks the question with an asterisk if he requires an oral answer, and for these he must give notice *at least* one day before the answer is required. He cannot insist on an answer to a question. A minister may always plead the public interest as his ground. Furthermore some questions are inadmissible—for example, those relating to grants of honours, the prerogative of mercy, the Royal Family, or questions which are "trivial vague and meaningless" or "seeking an expression of opinion". A minister need answer only for actions for which he is

[1] 3rd Rept. Sel. Comm. Procedure, para. 7.
[2] An average of between 72 and 74 days.
[3] *Op. cit.*, para. 6.   [4] *Op. cit.*, p. xxx.

constitutionally responsible, so that for years the actions of the Bank of England could not be queried. Recently the Government held that ministers were not responsible for the day-to-day operations of nationalized industries,[1] and that they need not answer questions bearing on these. But the range of questions asked is amazing. A "Hansard" picked up at random shows that on 2 February 1948, 51 questions were answered orally (and another 70 by writing) ranging over "passengers' service Larne-Stranraer" "laid-up tankers" and "cat's eye studs" to "ministerial responsibility for steel allocation".

A distinguished American observer[2] comments: "One may observe that the frequent triviality of the questions is beyond dispute. On the other hand it offers an opportunity to bring to immediate public attention any phase of administrative policy or activity. However while many of these questions are used to call the bureaucracy to account, many others are simply used to pester the group in power and to search out weak points for partisan criticism." This seems to play down many important features. The all pervasive character of questioning is one—everything and anything is covered in the course of a week or so. The effect on government departments is another. It is prodigious—at a question

"gelidusque per ima cucurrit ossa tremor"

"Anybody who has ever worked in a Civil Service Department," said Hugh Gaitskell[3] "would agree with me that if there is one major thing which leads Civil Servants to be excessively cautious, timid and careful and to keep records which outside the Civil Service would be regarded as unnecessary, it is the fear of the Parliamentary question". Then again, the question can, and usually is, followed by a series of supplementary questions designed to catch the Minister off his balance, to reply not in the sober words with which his civil servants have provided him, but extempore. Nor are the possible consequences of one seemingly trivial question stressed—the "unsatisfactory reply", the notice to "move it on the adjournment", the matter taken up formally by the Opposition in a full dress debate. And finally, it is certainly "pestering the group in power"—but what could be more desirable when they wield so extensive an authority? The instrument is flexible, quick, immediate

[1] Hansard, 2 Feb., 1948, col. 1453, 1822-28, also 3 March, 1948.
[2] P. Herring, *Presidential Leadership*, Farrar and Rinehart, 1939, p. 95.
[3] Hansard, 21 Oct., 1947, col. 74.

141

—and though strong enough to discredit, it is not strong enough to kill.

"Unsatisfactory" replies may be "raised on the adjournment" and this is another useful instrument of day-to-day control. To debate the adjournment of the House is an excuse for initiating a general debate, unlike a substantive motion where the debate must keep within the bounds of strict relevance. Sometimes therefore when the House wishes for a debate to range especially far and wide it will prefer to move the adjournment rather than a substantive motion. This is fairly rare. In its more usual context, the "adjournments" occur on the eve of recesses, whether at the weekends (when they take place on Fridays) or at the Xmas, Whitsun, Easter and Summer recesses (when one or even two days may be devoted to them). In addition, unless the S.O.s are suspended to allow Government business to be debated after 10.30 p.m. the half hour between 10.30 and 11 p.m. is devoted to adjournment debates. A member wishing to debate a matter gives formal notice to the Speaker and ballots for the opportunity. He may be unlucky, and draw a date only after so long a lapse of time that the point of the debate has passed. Adjournment debates of this kind must never deal with a matter such that new legislation would have to be passed, and they are not pressed to a division. Thus they tend always to deal with administration, to wound and not to kill. They can be highly embarassing to Ministers.

For specially urgent matters there is the so-called urgency procedure under S.O.8 which permits of debate that very day if a Member, supported by 40 others, moves the adjournment of the House on a matter of "definite urgent and public importance", and the Speaker accepts. This acts like a bombshell on front benches for Ministers have to speak with only a few hours coaching in the question. The Savidge Case of 1928 arose from an unsatisfactory answer to a question. The debate was held that night, the police actions which formed its subject were found highly discreditable and the matter was closed only by the Government promising to set up a Commission to enquire into the whole matter of police investigations. When Mr Bevin stated that the Government proposed to evacuate Egypt Mr Churchill moved the adjournment and the Speaker accepted it.[1] Similarly when the Government arrested members of the Jewish Agency, Mr Silverman moved the adjournment and Mr Speaker accepted the motion.[2] But such occasions are rare because the Speaker interprets "urgency", "public" and

[1] 7 May 1946.
[2] 1 July 1946.

"definiteness" very precisely and conservatively and it is seldom that such motions are accepted more than once or twice in a year.

Every action may provoke a question, every question an adjournment debate, and every adjournment a full dress debate. The discrediting of the Labour Government over the Fuel Crisis of Xmas 1946-7 began when Mr Blackburn raised the question of Messrs Austin's fuel supplies on an adjournment debate one Friday.[1] There are many occasions for such full dress debates, and the topics are chosen by the Opposition, not the Government. They are generally concerned with policy rather than detail, but the opportunity for raising detail is always there, and furthermore, if they are running a good hare, the Opposition can put down the motion again and again. The King's Speech is nearly always very general, as it revolves round the Government's proposed programme of legislation for the coming session. The 26 Supply days which are now spread over the whole session provide the chief opposition opportunities. The debates take place on the Estimates. But any matter can be raised under the appropriate estimate and the Opposition can debate the same estimate over the whole 26 days if it chooses. The choice is entirely in its hands. Usually the selection is very varied and turns more on policy than administration. But give them a good scandal and an Opposition can thoroughly discredit the Government. Finally there are substantive motions which, at the Opposition's request, the Government accepts outside the normal supply days. These are motions so couched that the Government cannot for shame refuse. A vote of censure for example is one which no Government will decline however crowded the session.[2] By question and debate, all administration, in detail and in the large, is kept under a constant and ceaseless review, where the most trivial detail may be fraught with enormous consequences, where the Opposition spends its whole time seeking the Executive's weak point, and having once found it, has boundless opportunities to hammer and hammer away, constantly keeping it before the public eye. Opposition works not through swaying voters in the division lobbies, but through swaying potential voters in the next general election: and that election is the sanction of what the Government is prepared to fight or prepared to yield on. For this purpose the procedure of the Commons is marvellously organized.

[1] 7 February 1947.
[2] Cf. *especially* Mr Morrison's experiences, 3rd Report Sel. Comm. Estimates, Q. 3241.

On choosing subjects for attack, the Opposition is often influenced and informed by the Reports of the Special Committees, set up each year, viz. the Public Accounts Committee and the Select Committee on Estimates. Their work is so exclusively concerned with administrative detail as to warrant some mention. Furthermore, their recommendations usually carry great weight because they are always liable to debate. The Public Accounts Committee's task[1] is to examine the Report of the Comptroller's Auditor General and to make recommendations thereon to the House. Since it is assisted by the C.A.G.s staff it can work fairly cogently and speedily. The Treasury reply to the recommendations in Minutes which are also made public. The bulk of the recommendations not unnaturally revolve around financial matters but these so often have important administrative bearings that the "Epitome of the Reports"[2] is a vital source for all administrative departments from 1857 when the Committee was first set up. The "grilling" of Civil Servants by the Committee, which probes very deeply into administrative practices, is itself a powerful engine of control, a "real factor in administration".[3]

The Select Committee of Estimates, set up in its present form in 1912 was originally intended to examine the current estimates for the year in order to give the House advice before they were debated. In fact it has to limit itself to one or two sets of estimates and even then it does not conclude reporting till a year later, when the Estimates have been not only voted but spent. Thus it is as retrospective as the P.A.C. Before 1939, its reports were of little significance. During the War both P.A.C. and Estimates Committee were suspended and their place taken by a Committee on National Expenditure. This took its duties very seriously, visiting ministries, camps and factories, pressing departments for immediate memoranda, and producing a series of reports of great power and formidable influence. When the Select Committees were restored to their pre-war form the Estimates Committee continued this vigorous tradition. It is almost uniquely responsible, for example, for the recent development or O.M. work.

Since the P.A.C. and the Estimates Committee tend both to work on accounts and both stray beyond the limits of the financial year in which they are interested, the Select Committee on Procedure suggested their amalgamation. Sir Gilbert Campion went somewhat further, suggesting that they should be served with a permanent

[1] See p. 56
[2] H.C. 154 of 1938.
[3] Sel. Comm. Procedure, H. Morrison, Q. 3227.

staff. Both concurred in suggesting that two days be specially put aside for debating its reports.

The Government rejected the proposals. Mr Herbert Morrison made no secret of the fact that he thought the Committee would be far too powerful. "A system", said the Government Memorandum[1], "which subjected every item of departmental expenditure over a three year period to the close and searching scrutiny of a small body of members would place a very heavy burden on senior officers and inevitably hamper the efficiency of executive action by importing delays and cramping initiative." Mr Morrison elaborated. He said that the Government was anxious not to repeat the "difficulties caused by the Committee of National Expenditure." This Committee he alleged, were sometimes actually, "overhauling current executive activities", sometimes recommending an *increase* in expenditure, and on other occasions asking the Civil Service questions "which in the judgment of some of the Ministers at that time were so to speak running rival with the executive responsibility of the Minister himself."[2] He feared that the proposed new Committee would also "drop on departments on current activities"; that this was undesirable because it not only took up the time of Civil Servants but made them "lose their nerve"[3]: that Sir Gilbert Campion's suggestion of staffing the Committee with trained clerks was to create a "rival administrative set-up in the Palace of Westminster side by side with Whitehall"[4] and that this sent[5] "shivers down the back of Whitehall"[6]. "Who," he demanded "is responsible for executive current administration? The Government or Parliament? I say it is the Government. ... "[7] Mr Morrison's evidence is one of the finest commentaries yet made on the implications of Cabinet government and ministerial responsibility. The primacy of the Executive could not have been expounded more explicitly.[8]

Its primacy is also implied in Parliament's delegation of subordinate law making to Ministers. This vexed problem is only now in the process of solution.

It has been stressed already that few statutes are so complete as to allow no dispute at all as to their precise meaning in individual cases. In the nineteenth century the further definition of the statute

---

[1] Sel. Comm., p. 99. [2] Q. 3229.
[3] Q. 3245. [4] Q. 3260. [5] Q. 3277.
[6] Cf. also Q. 3270—where the "trained clerks" were regarded by Whitehall as "sleuths ... trying to trip them up".
[7] Q. 3260. [8] See Book I, Chapter 3.

was largely left to the Court, and case-law filled in the imprecise details.[1] The last half century has seen a twin process, the statutes becoming less and less precise, and their elaboration being delegated, not to case-law, but to the responsible ministries in the form of Rules, Orders and Regulations—what are now known as Statutory Instruments. Thus a "parent" statute is passed by Parliament laying down the general lines of the law, but formally delegating to the Minister a power to fill in detail by regulations under the Act. Sometimes, as under the Emergency Powers Act of 1939, the Act sanctions not only delegation in the form of Orders-in-Council containing Defence Regulations but sub-delegation also, in the form of "orders, rules and bye-laws". Sometimes there emerges what has been called[2] "a pedigree of 5 generations", viz. the Statute, the Defence Regulations made under the Statute, the Orders made under the Defence Regulations, the Directions made under the Orders and the licences issued under the Directions. It sounds like "The King of Caractacus has just passed along—"

The increase of such sub-legislation is not nearly so recent as has been pretended in some quarters. Excluding war years there has been a fairly steady average since (significantly) the social legislation of the Liberal Government of 1906. Nor is the *extent* of regulation so novel as critics make it appear. The Quarter Sessions of the eighteenth and nineteenth centuries, composed of nominated gentry, who exercised control over the counties and their parishes, issued thousands and thousands of regulations; as these were often in the form of verbal instructions or court-orders, as the Quar .. r Sessions was technically a Court and its J.P.s Magistrates, as, finally they were considered as hereditarily entitled to their powers, the Common-lawyer of the twentieth century ignores the existence of such "regimentation".[3] As the J.P.s and their successors the modern local authorities were brought into a closer dependence on the Central Government, the task of issuing such directions naturally fell upon its Ministries.

---

[1] See e.g. the fate of rating of machinery and railways in the House of Lords, Finer, *Local Government*, p. 401 *et seq.*

[2] 3rd Special Report from Sel. Comm. S.R.O.s, 29 Oct., 1946, p. 7.

[3] What is more, as Maitland or Keir and Lawson have pointed out (*q.v. Cases in Constitutional Law*) these bodies mixed administrative and judicial functions together. It is no wonder therefore that as the Central Ministries have superseded so many of the regulatory powers of Quarter Sessions, they too should exercise a similarly administrative-cum-judicial set of unctions.

Now in peacetime the local S.R.O.s "balance or outnumber the general" in 1927 for instance there were nearly twice as many local S.R.O. as general S.R.O. and in 1926 nearly three times as many."[1] and in 1937 nearly equal proportions. The growth of at least *half* the number of our S.R.O.s is thus accounted for by a simple switch of functions from local bodies to central ones—which in view of all that has been said above may offend but hardly perplex. The *general* S.R.O.s represent a switch from law-making by the Courts to *formal* law-making by departments. The case for such a transference was made with conclusive force by the Committee on Ministers' Powers of 1932.[2] Flexibility, and the speed with which emergencies can be met are its keynotes. "It can limit the applicability of legislation by time, location, ownership, age or otherwise and all these limitations are able to be changed at short notice." The decisions are political not judicial, and ones which "only a legislative is competent to take". "Where a legislature is forced to influence the economic life of the country by physical measures, powers of this kind are almost inevitable."[3]

These Orders, Rules and Regulations however are made in pursuance of an Act of Parliament, they are subordinate law—and consequently, it is argued, Parliament should scrutinize and approve what is in fact the *use* made by the Executive of Parliamentary powers. Now in point of fact Parliament does not always stand on such a right. The greater majority of Instruments which are made do not have to be shown to Parliament ("laid" on the Desk is the technical term). Of those which must be laid, there is a class for which no further Parliamentary Action is envisaged. This is entirely a matter for Parliament—it controls such arrangements by its control of the Parent Statute which describes them. The more important S.R.O.s however—and it is with these that the argument now deals—*are* subject to proceedings. They must be affirmed positively, by resolutions of both Houses—this usually for the most important; or negatively, i.e. they are considered approved if after "lying" for 40 days, neither House has passed a resolution to annul.

The machinery of control is three-fold, viz. the arrangements to secure that instruments are in fact laid before the House, their scrutiny by a Select Committee, and the arrangements for contesting

---

[1] Sel. Comm. Procedure, p. 243.
[2] Cmd. 4060 of 1932, at section II, para 11.
[3] Mr Hugh Molson, Hansard, 17 May, 1944.

them. The first is necessary because an Order takes legal effect as soon as it is published,[1] irrespective as to whether it has been laid, *providing* that the Ministry have told the Lord Chancellor and the Speaker of the House that it is essential for the instrument to come into force immediately. It used to be possible for a Ministry to withhold the instrument for ever, by alleging such urgency (i.e. by declaring it a "provisional rule"). The law therefore provides that all instruments required to be laid by their Parent Act *must* be so laid "before the instrument comes into operation", unless breaches of this rule are first explained to the Speaker and Lord Chancellor and that each instrument when printed must carry a legend stating when it came into operation or will do so and also when it was laid, and when it *will* be.[2]

This enables any interested M.P. to draw the attention of the House to the fact that the law has not been complied with: and such a function has now been vested since 1944 in a Select Committee on S.R. and O.s. Its terms of reference exclude any judgments on the *merits* of an Order. It must draw the attention of the House to any instruments which (i) Impose a charge on public revenues, (ii) exclude the challenge of the courts, (iii) make unexpected and unusual use of the powers conferred by the parent statute,[3] (iv) call for elucidation by reason of their form and purpose and (v) have been subject to unjustifiable delay in publication and presentation to Parliament.

Once laid the Order may be subject to either affirmative resolution, or to annulment. The motion to annul takes the form of a "prayer" moved by a Member. Such "prayers" are not in Government time and consequently cannot be suppressed by the Whip's control of the time table. They are "exempted business", i.e. taken after 10.30 when the House customarily adjourns, and they can go on as long as the member moving the prayer can keep a quorum of the House together.

Certain critics of delegated legislation have declared such control to be wholly insufficient. Mr C. K. Allen for instance has made a number of suggestions. First, he would like to see the Select Committee organized into sub-committees, and certainly there is need

[1] Statutory Instruments Act, 9 and 10, Geo. VI, 3 (i) and (ii).

[2] 9 and 10 Geo. VI, cap. 4.

[3] The view was privately expressed by a distinguished Parliamentary authority that this term of reference is wide enough for the Committee to extend its investigations to *policy*—if it so wished. So far, however, it has strictly adhered to review of form rather than substance.

for some strengthening along these lines, for the Committee is overwhelmed with its work. He further suggests that prayers should be moved to amend, as well as to annul. This is highly desirable but for the moment not practicable, because many of the most important Orders must become operative *before* they are laid: consequent amendment would cause administrative chaos. Next he proposes that the Committee should have power to scrutinize the parent statutes and report to the House on the subordinate law making powers they confer: but this seems an unnecessary reduplication of the work of the Standing Committees. Finally, in company with the Clerk of the House he proposes that the Committee report on the merits of the Orders and have power to enquire into grievances. These last two proposals met with almost unanimous condemnation from the other witnesses called by the Select Committee on Procedure, and yet found favour with the Committee itself. The Government's reply seems to me unanswerable: "The first[1] would mean that Ministers would have to attend before the Select Committee to defend the policy embodied in subordinate legislation: the second would have the effect of enabling the Select Committee to enquire into all phases of Government administration within the very wide field covered by delegated legislation."[2] To the first consideration Sir Cecil Carr added[3] "it raises such important administrative considerations that the Government might feel obliged to prepare itself to resist challenge on party lines and the present impartial scrutiny would change its character." As to the second he commented:

"Cases of hardship may arise by hundreds if not thousands. How are they to be sifted? Will every discontented motorist be allowed to complain of the application of the Control of Motor Fuel Order? ... A single petitioner appearing in person might well occupy more than a day's sitting; organizations representing trades and industries might occupy several days ... It will be difficult to deal with particular cases without study of official correspondence and perhaps departmental files; will these be made available ... ?"[4]

The truth appears to me to be that many of the critics wish to extend the control of the House for deep and not explicit reasons. ... The lawyer objects, quite rightly to the barbarous draughtsmanship, the opacity of language, the unconsolidated nature of too many of

---

[1] Proposed additional function. [2] Sel. Comm. 3rd Rept. p. 100.
[3] *Ibid.*, p. 244 [4] *Ibid.*

these Orders. But many also object to clouds of regulations because they object to "regulation and controls". The statutory instrument brings government home to the governed—it occurs at the actual point of making law, *fact*. Now in very many cases, the ministry which executes the law has itself, by means of its orders and regulations, interpreted what it would like to suppose the law may mean: and in *some* cases it does so in such a way that appeal to the courts is *excluded*. The critic argues that *if* the courts may not interpret, then the legislature must. Otherwise the Ministry makes up its own interpretation, applies it to individual cases and executes its own decision. The three powers of Montesquieu are confounded and liberty has perished.

The demand for further Parliamentary scrutiny thus becomes the sharper as judicial scope for reviewing the Orders and Regulations disappears. To what extent may the Courts then interfere?

CHAPTER 3

JUDICIAL CONTROL OF THE ADMINISTRATION

*"If the Reader fairly considers the strength of what I have advanced
in the foregoing section, I am convinced it will have produced a
wonderful Revolution in his Notions and Opinions; And he will be
abundantly better prepared to receive and to relish the concluding part
of this Miraculous Treatise—"*

Swift: A Compliment to the Readers.

THE Civil Service is an instrument to carry out public *will*, and
this will is expressed by Parliament in the form of law. The
actions of the civil servant may therefore be challenged by any
individual either by taking up the matter with the body which
makes the law, i.e. Parliament, or the body which traditionally says
what the law *means*, viz. the Courts.

The Courts will take action if the plaintiff can show that the law
confers an obligation on the civil servant which he has failed to
carry out. It may also take action if the plaintiff can show that no
law in fact obliged the civil servant to act as he has done, and he has
therefore acted without any *authority*. The first class of complaint
allows a plaintiff to sue, not just the individual civil servant, but the
Department itself, either for breaches of contract, or for that class of
civil wrongs which are designated "torts". A special procedure
was used for breaches of contract, where the plaintiff sued by
Petition of Right. This was within the power of the Attorney
General to withhold but it was never in fact withheld. Until 1948, it
was only possible to sue the Crown in tort by a complicated legal
fiction (though there were no such difficulties in the way of suing
local authorities). Since the Crown Procedure Act of 1947, proceedings against the Crown in tort and contract are assimilated
to the procedure of one subject versus another. These matters are
as straightforward as any legal matter can be, and this chapter does
not deal with them any further. It is devoted to the second class of
cases where the plaintiff alleges that the Civil Servant has acted
without any authority, i.e. *ultra vires*, and that his action is thereby
null and void.

The law makes a distinction between purely executive duties conferred on civil servants and those which involve "arbitration", or "having to adjudicate between two or more parties".[1] "In the case of the administrative decision there is no legal obligation upon the person charged with the duty of reaching the decision to consider and weigh submissions and arguments, or to collate any evidence, or to solve any issue. The grounds upon which he acts, and the means which he takes to inform himself before acting are left entirely to his discretion".[2] A purely executive decision—say the placing of a contract, or the naturalization of an alien—may be set aside by the Courts, because in scope, form, or purpose it exceeds the powers conferred on the Civil Servant. A judicial (or "quasi-judicial") decision may be set aside by the Courts if they hold that the Civil Servant is outside the powers the law confers on him, in the sense that although it requires him to render a "judicial" decision, he has not in fact, acted "judicially". In all these cases the courts may hold that he has acted *ultra vires*—"beyond his powers".

Sometimes the two—executive and judicial decisions—are found mixed up as part of one process. The Local Government Act of 1933 empowers the Minister of Health to make a compulsory purchase Order: such Orders compel an owner to sell his land, the price being fixed by an independent valuer. If the owner objects, the Minister must make the confirmation of the Order depend on the outcome of a Local Enquiry held by one of his Inspectors. Such an Enquiry is *judicial* in character and hence the Minister must be able to prove to a Court that he conducted it "judicially"—a term whose imprecise meaning is elaborated later. Providing he has done this, the subsequent steps which the Minister takes relating to publicity of the Order, maps of the area in question and its final confirmation, are strictly *executive*.

This executive act might be *ultra vires* by *scope*, where, for instance, the Order relates to the compulsory purchase of cattle and the Parent Act mentions only land. It might be *ultra vires* by form, if for instance the Minister failed to give the exact kind of publicity demanded by the Parent Act. Finally it might be *ultra vires* by purpose—the Act may make sale compulsory for town planning purposes, but the order may in fact have been made for the private use of a member of a local council.

[1] Law Reports 1948, Pt. 1, January. Franklin and Others *v.* Min. of Town and Country Planning.
[2] Committee on Ministers' Powers, Cmd. 4060 of 1932.

This seems fairly straightforward, but difficulties arose where the Parent Acts were found to contain clauses apparently designed to exclude review by the Courts. One such clause ran "shall be conclusive evidence that the requirements of this Act shall have been complied with, and that the order has been duly made and is within the powers of this Act." The other ran that rules and regulations "shall have effect as if enacted in this Act". Both cases were affected by a decision given in Yaffe's Case (Rex v. Ministry of Health, Ex.p. Yaffe, 1931). Unfortunately the part of the judgment bearing on the interpretation of these clauses was not the "reason of the decision" (the *ratio decidendi*) but a *dictum* of the Lords, and this is not legally binding though it has enormous authority. However the Courts have since largely acted on this interpretation. The Lords' dictum was, that such classes did *not* preclude the Courts from enquiring whether the orders and regulations made under an Act conflicted with that Act: i.e. they could review such orders to see if they were *ultra vires* in any of the three senses mentioned above.

The present position is therefore that in cases concerning purely executive decisions, the Courts may ask and decide whether or not the action taken was or was not within the power of the Minister. If they decide it was *intra vires*, then within that jurisdiction the Minister may act freely. The Courts thus draw their *own* line as to where they may take cognizance: and over that line, i.e. beyond the jurisdiction they circumscribe around themselves, the Minister is free to act. This was illustrated by the Stevenage Case.[1] Here the House of Lords held that when the Minister made an Order under the New Towns Act, he was exercising a purely executive function delegated to him by Parliament. They found that he had done so in the form prescribed in the Statute. Whether he *should* have done so, and whether the Court would have done as he did was neither here nor there. That was the Minister's responsibility. A somewhat similar line of reasoning underlies Liveridge v. Anderson, 1941. The Home Secretary was given a power to detain individuals if he had "reasonable cause to believe" them to be of "hostile origin or associations". The Lords held that Parliament had clearly conferred on the Home Secretary an absolute discretion in making up his mind. That being so it was not for the Court to decide what it would have done if *it* had had to decide the case of Liveridge. If within his powers to do, the wisdom or unwisdom of the Minister's action is not within the

[1] Franklin and Others v. Min. of Town and Country Planning, 1948—Appeal to House of Lords.

purview of the Courts: not so the decision as to whether the action is within his powers. This is for the Court to decide. Review therefore may become—as it did on the 18*b* regulations—a very restricted thing.[1]

When however a *judicial* power is conferred on the Minister other considerations arise, viz. "Natural Justice". For if the Act says or implies he must act judicially and it can be shown that he has not, then he has acted *beyond* the powers conferred in the Statute.

The two former Chapters have shown how such judicial powers have come to be conferred on primarily Executive bodies. Chapter 1 showed how accountability was transferred from Parliament to a self acting process within the Agency itself such as the appeal tribunals of the U.A.B.—how, so to speak, certain administrative agencies became judicialized. Chapter 2 showed how Parliament conferred on Departments a right to fill in the general clauses of Statutes by sub-legislation. Now, in the nineteenth century, the imprecisions of a Statute would have been filled in by case-law, i.e. judicial interpretation. When Parliament permits the Department to make subordinate laws, it is transferring the right to interpret a Statute away from the Courts to the Departments, whose interpretation takes the form of Rules and Orders. Parliament may go even further. It may vest the right of interpreting these interpretative orders themselves in the Tribunals or in the Minister himself. For example the Minister of Education alone has jurisdiction over disputes arising between two local authorities. Finally Parliament may vest this right of interpretation *exclusively* in the Minister or his Tribunals, by making their decision legally final and excluding appeal to the Courts. There is no appeal from the decision of the Assistance Board's Appeal Tribunals. Cases arising under the Unemployment Assistance Acts go from the Minister's Court of Referees to an Umpire, himself a Ministerial appointment, whose decision is final. There is an automatic right of appeal from the Traffic Commissioners' decision in public service matters but to the Minister, not the Courts. A Rent Tribunal can fix a rent and a landlord cannot get a Court of law to review the substance of its decision.

These Tribunals are very numerous,[2] and they vary extensively among themselves. There is no uniformity as to personnel. Most members of the Courts of Referees are lawyers, but recently many laymen have been appointed. Not one of the full-time Traffic

[1] C. K. Allen, *Law and Orders*, p. 303.

[2] Robson's *Justice and Administrative Law*, Chapter 2.

Commissioners is a lawyer. The Committees which the Ministry of Health appoints to consider patients' complaints against their panel doctors, consist of one lawyer and two doctors. Secondly, there is no uniformity as to procedure. Some take evidence in writing only: others, like the Rent Tribunals, conduct their hearing orally. Nearly all decline to publish the evidence or report on which their decision was founded. This makes cross-examination, or rebuttal evidence farcical. Others decline to give reasons for their decisions, like the Conscientious Objectors' Tribunals, but some do, like the Road Traffic Commissioners. In some Tribunals—for example in every one of the Ministry of Labour's Tribunals, with the exception of their Reinstatement Committee—the citizen may not be represented by counsel. Many a citizen not unnaturally resents such oddities. To be tried by a strange unformalized procedure, unable to cross examine or rebut the opposing party, sometimes denied an oral hearing and, where this is permitted, denied the use of a lawyer— this is bad enough. When the case finally goes against him and he is denied a reason for that decision, he may well think it intolerable. The law prohibits appeal to the Law Courts: the question obviously arises whether, despite the "finality" of such Tribunals, there is not some way of getting the Courts to intervene. And in fact there is— in all cases the plaintiff may plead that he has "not had a fair trial". Legally the plea is expressed as a "denial of natural justice". If he can get the Court to accept this plea, the Tribunal's decision is *ultra vires*, and is quashed as null and void.

To the Courts Natural Justice implies first, that there must be no *bias*—the Tribunal must decide fairly and impartially. Secondly, a party must be given fair notice of the case against him and a chance to be heard in his own defence. Lastly, the power of the Tribunal may not be used for an improper purpose—Land may not be acquired compulsorily when ostensibly it is acquired for a housing scheme but really to make profits for the municipality. Now not one of these considerations is very precise, and so a great deal of latitude has been left to the Courts: and so here again, the Courts draw their *own* lines of jurisdiction. If they interpreted "natural justice" to mean the kind of procedure adopted by courts of law, they would be able to intervene very widely indeed. In point of fact they have closely restricted their intervention, by the leading case of Arlidge *v.* Local Government Board (1914). In this case, the Local Government Board after holding a local enquiry, had confirmed a compulsory purchase order for some of Arlidge's properties. Arlidge complained that the action was supposedly judicial yet denied him natural justice, for he did not know the clerk who had finally decided to confirm the order, the enquiry had not been conducted orally and he had been denied access to the Inspector's report on which the judgment had been founded. The House of Lords held that he had no right to expect any such procedure. "The decision must be come to in the spirit and with the sense of responsibility of a tribunal whose duty it is to mete out justice. But it does not follow that the procedure of every such tribunal must be the same."[1]"That the judiciary should presume to impose its own methods on administrative or executive officers is an usurpation—"[2] The result of this far reaching decision has been to multiply the countless varieties of constitution and procedure in the Administrative tribunals.

Thus the Courts will certainly entertain any objection to the procedures and constitution of administrative tribunals, but they interpret "natural justice" in a sense very liberal to the executive. Now, once allowed to be "judicial", the tribunal is within its powers, and the Courts will not review in any further way the use it makes of those powers. It will not substitute its judgment for theirs.

There still remains one final question however. An aggrieved individual may appeal to a Law Court on the grounds that he has been denied natural justice: but this presupposes that the powers conferred on the Minister or Tribunal are judicial. If it can be shown that those powers are purely executive, then no case will lie. The Courts therefore must entertain a third class of problem—viz. *is* the power conferred to be considered Executive or Judicial? This is often extremely difficult to discern. Consider the Stevenage Cases. Under the New Towns Act the Minister may make an Order designating particular areas as the site of a New Town. If any objections be made, he is also bound to hold a public local enquiry. The Minister prepared a draft Order which designated Stevenage as such a site. When the plaintiffs made objection, he ordered one of his Inspectors to hold the public local enquiry. The Inspector did so, and submitted a complete transcript of the proceedings to the Minister who thereupon *confirmed* his Draft Order.

Franklin, the plaintiff, demanded of the High Court that the Order be quashed (a) because it was *ultra vires* the Act of 1946 and (b) because (i) the Minister had been biased inasmuch as he had stated before the Order was made that he *intended* to make it;

[1] A.C. 120; 38 Digest, 217, p. 132.
[2] *Ibid. loc. cit.* p. 138.

(ii) that the local enquiry was held *after* the draft Order and not before and (iii) the Minister had neither fairly nor properly considered the objections or given fair and proper effect to the result or such considerations.

In the High Court, Justice Henn Collins held that although the Order was *intra vires* the Act, it was a denial of justice. At the Enquiry evidence had been put forward to show that the water and sewerage problems of Stevenage could not be met, and this evidence had not been rebutted. The Minister had thereby proved, said Mr Collins, that he intended to make the Order *whatever* the weight of the objections. The implication here was that the local enquiry was judicial in character and the Minister had acted injudicially. The Order was quashed. An appeal to the Master of the Rolls also implied that the power was a judicial one—but held it had been properly exercised, and did *not* show bias. The judgment of the Lower Court was quashed. The appellants appealed to the House of Lords. The Lords upheld the Master of the Rolls but for a quite different reason. They stated that the power was *not* judicial but executive. The local enquiry was simply "for the further information of the respondent, in order to the final consideration of the soundness of the scheme of the designation."[1] The only question was whether the Minister had complied "with the statutory discretions to appoint a person to hold the public enquiry, and to consider that person's report". This, the Court said, he had done. The order was consequently valid!

The Courts then, will review any cases where the Statute explicitly allows appeal to the High Court. Even in those cases where no such right of appeal is permitted the Courts may always determine whether or no the actions performed were legal in scope, purpose and form, and in the case of judicial discretion, if it was also conformable to natural justice. Therefore they have also to decide which kind of discretion was in fact conferred. In practice the Courts have limited their own jurisdiction very considerably in all these matters. The citizen is more and more faced with a situation where he cannot raise his grievances in the House or in the ordinary Courts of Law.

The remedy is necessary and the path reasonably clear and the American Administrative Procedure Act can in many ways prove a model. It is to standardize and liberalize the administrative tribunals, as far as this is possible. The American Act has separated the judicial and executive powers of the Tribunals by first, making the

[1] The Law Reports, Pt. 1, January 1948, Appeal Cases, p. 102.

examiner or inspector *decide* on the enquiry he has just held but giving the aggrieved party an appeal to the Minister or Board itself: it ensures that the local examiners or inspectors are not engaged in active administration by segregating them from the active administrators' work, giving them a judicial tenure and laying it down that they take their cases in a fixed rota. Secondly it has liberalized the procedure by allowing any aggrieved party the right to be heard orally, to be represented by counsel, and to submit rebuttal evidence. The last carries with it the implication that the facts on which the decision has been based should be made available to him. These reforms are widely applicable in this country and so is the further requirement that the reasons for decisions should be made known—although it would be necessary to make it clear that the administrative tribunal is *not* bound by its former decision. It is true that these remedies will not always be applicable in all cases. For example, there are often excellent reasons why an Inspector's report should not be made public. When the remedies do not apply however the onus must be upon the Ministry to show good cause why not. Since Administrative Justice is here to stay it must be liberalized and unified and made to combine the flexibility and fertility of administrative inventiveness with the liberties of the citizen.

BIBLIOGRAPHY

For a general view of the nature of administration in modern Democracies the reader may consult H. Finer, *Theory and Practice of Modern Government*, Methuen, 1932. France is covered by the three volumes of Taine's *Le Régime Moderne*, Hachette; and by W. R. Sharp's *Government of the French Republic*, Van Nostrand and Co., 1939. The U.S.A. by Beard's *American Government and Politics*, Macmillan, 1942; Leonard White's *Introduction to the Study of Public Administration*, Macmillan, 1944; and *Recent Social Trends*, the Report of the President's Committee on Social Trends, McGraw Hill Book Company, 1932.

The principles of British Government are covered in a manner explained by the titles, in Dicey's classic, *Law of the Constitution*, Macmillan, 9th edition, 1947; Jennings' *Law and the Constitution*, a brilliant critique of Dicey's work. The central government is described in Sir Ivor Jennings's two volumes, *Parliament*, C.U.P., 1939, and *Cabinet Government*, C.U.P., 1936; in H. J. Laski's *Parliamentary Government in England*, Allen and Unwin, 1938; and in the luminous essays of the Rt. Hon. L. S. Amery's *Thoughts on the Constitution*, Macmillan, 1947. A work of the greatest importance in describing the role of Parliament is the *Third Report and Minutes of Evidence of the Select Committee on Procedure, 1946*.

The problems arising from the construction of Departments may be studied from the *Report of the Machinery of Government Committee* (the "Haldane Report"), H.M.S.O., 1918; and in the penetrating work of Professor Schuyler Wallace, *Federal Departmentalization*, Columbia University Press, 1941.

The Treasury is well described in Sir Charles Heath's *The Treasury*, Putnams, 1900; while a remarkable amount of information which is still relevant and many important historical documents, are to be found in the *Report of the Committee on National Expenditure of 1902*. Recent developments in the Treasury's supervisory role, especially as regards "organization and methods", are treated in the *16th Report of the Committee of National Expenditure of 1942*, the *14th Report of 1943*, the *4th Report of 1940*, and the *5th Report of the Select Committee of Estimates, 1947*. Similarly, some aspects of interdepartmental co-operation are admirably illustrated in the *5th Report of the Select Committee on Estimates of 1945-6* (Sub-Committee C, the Housing Estimates), and the *2nd Report of the Committee for 1946-7* (Development Areas).

Local government has a large literature and at the time of going to press nearly all the classical works have been brought up to date and reprinted. Among the best are H. Finer's *English Local Government*, new edition, Methuen, 1949; Robson's *Development of Local Government*, Allen and Unwin, 2nd edition, 1948; and Warren's *Municipal Administration*, Pitman, 1948. Page, *Co-ordination and Planning in the Local Authority*, though ill-digested has some very useful information. V. D. Lipson's *Local Government Areas* (B. Blackwell, 1949) is a remarkable work on the "Boundary Problem".

The British Civil Service can be studied in H. Finer's essay *The British Civil Service*, Allen and Unwin, 1937; and in H. R. Greaves's *The Civil Service in the Changing State*, Allen and Unwin, 1948; but for an account of the daily round of the administrator the reader's attention is especially directed to Dale's *The Higher Civil Service* and Sir Oliver Franks's *Experiences of a University Professor in the Civil Service* and in the *9th Report of the Select Committee of Estimates, 1947*.

Finally the vexed question of administrative law and its relation to delegated legislation is considered in Sir Cecil Carr's *Concerning English Administrative Law*, O.U.P.; Professor Robson's *Justice and Administrative Law*, Stevens, 1948; and C. K. Allen's *Law and Orders*, Stevens, 1945.